EXTRAORDINARY ENDANGERED ANIMALS

By Sandrine Silhol and Gaëlle Guérive
Illustrations by Marie Doucedame

Abrams Books for Young Readers
New York

Cataloging-in-Publication Data has been applied for and may be obtained from the Library of Congress.
ISBN 978-1-4197-0034-7

Text copyright © 2011 Sandrine Sihol and Gaëlle Guérive
Illustrations copyright © 2011 Marie Doucedame

Book design by Meagan Bennett

Printed and bound in Spain
10 9 8 7 6 5 4 3 2 1

115 West 18th Street
New York. NY 10011
www.abramsbooks.com

EXTRAORDINARY ENDANGERED ANIMALS

Contents

Introduction

Our lives are closely connected to those of the animals that surround us. The monkey is our cousin, we've domesticated the horse, the now-extinct aurochs has become the ox, the wolf has turned into our dog, the silkworm has given us beautiful clothes, and the maggot protects us from serious infections. We've identified roughly over a million animal species. Of those numbers, the International Union for Conservation of Nature's Red List indicates that close to 43,000 are endangered and face possible extinction.

Living in harmony with nature

Life on earth is the result of a subtle balance, one that gives us a great diversity of life. This "biodiversity" includes animals, plants, and fungi. The fragile balance is forged by the relationships among these three groups. Today, that balance is threatened by the rapid disappearance of many species. When a population is made up of only a few individuals scattered throughout the wild, males and females have trouble finding each other to reproduce. The species is then endangered, at risk of going extinct.

The animals discussed in this book are all facing that danger. They represent all endangered species, including the ones not mentioned here. Wild animals on every continent are harmed by mankind's growing influence as more and more people constantly encroach on nature to satisfy increasingly demanding lifestyles. If everyone on earth consumed as much as a European, we would need about three planets to live on. If everyone lived like an American, we would need five. But we only have one earth, and so we are not leaving much room for the animals.

Animals' natural habitats are being turned into fields, mines, and cities. In some areas, species are being introduced to habitats where they aren't normally found and where their proliferation can become uncontrollable and cause a major danger for other species. People are overhunting and overfishing to excess. Meanwhile, the effects of pollution and climate change are also damaging the environment. The threats are countless. It is urgent that we find a way to live in harmony with nature and all of its inhabitants.

Biodiversity: our "life insurance"

Fishermen, gatherers, hunters, farmers, and nomads are all seeing their lifestyles and traditional bearings deteriorate as animals disappear. Biodiversity is the source of food, medicine, raw materials, and services that work for us all, such as air purification, water filtering, climate stabilization, and flood control. But it is also where we draw the inspiration for the technologies of tomorrow, our modes of living and thinking, our dreams, and our appreciation of beauty.

Must all animals be protected?

Only 1,600 giant pandas remain on the planet. This peaceful bear has become a symbol for the protection of nature as a whole. It serves as a sign that all animals, including even the smallest, have their rightful place on earth. All play a specific role: predator, prey, beautiful, ugly, small, big, feathered, furry, scaly. . . . There are no "useful" and "useless" creatures. Even species we might like to get rid of have essential roles in relationship to other species.

As one example, the mole rat, a rodent that lives underground in places like California, seems like a waking nightmare to us. Picture a furless, wrinkled white rat, whose head has no visible eyes, nose, or ears, just two pointy teeth sticking out, and who spends all its time turning over soil. It manages to turn over 40 percent of the surface of its territory every year! But a fragile plant, the *Plantago erecta* or dwarf plantain, can grow only where the mole rat has done its work. And this plant is the only source of food for a magnificent threatened butterfly, the *Euphydryas editha* or bay checkerspot. Without that ugly little mole rat, there would be no beautiful butterfly.

A species' disappearance affects all animals relating to it in an ecosystem. For example, some rejoiced over the decline of sharks in U.S. waters. But these people hadn't thought about the fact that sharks eat other predators, such as crustaceans, that feed on shellfish. With fewer sharks, you have more crustaceans eating more shellfish. As a result, the annual harvest of shellfish dropped significantly, leaving much less for people to catch and eat.

No effort is useless

Protecting the Southwestern water vole, the California condor, the mountain tapir, and the tree kangaroo is a challenging but essential battle. And it isn't a waste of time: We already have the means to do it. We must look after their natural habitats, urge governments to modify laws, push corporations to use

production methods more respectful of the environment, encourage citizens to consume less and also consume more sensibly, and adopt lifestyles that agree with nature.

The means are within our reach. The simplest solutions consist of avoiding throwaway products, choosing to eat meals without meat from time to time, opting for notebooks made of recycled paper, and taking the time to understand the species that surround us without endangering them. Think about what the actress Betty Reese said: "If you think you are too small to be effective, you have never been in bed with a mosquito." Have you ever noticed how such a tiny creature can keep you up all night? Now it's our turn to keep the world from falling asleep while animals disappear. This book will show you what each of these animals can teach us.

Greenland

Alaska

Canada

NORTH AMERICA

United States

Mexico

Cuba

Dominican Republic

Haiti

Iceland

Norway

United Kingdom

Ireland   Germany

France

Portugal

Spain   Italy

Tunisia

Morocco

Western
Sahara

Algeria

Mauritania

Senegal   Mali   18

Nige

19

20   Nige

Ivory Coast   Cameroon

Gabon

Colombia   Venezuela

6

Ecuador

7   Brazil   **SOUTH AMERICA**

Peru

9

Bolivia   10

11   Paraguay

Chile

Argentina   Uruguay

1 Sea otter
2 California condor
3 Black-footed ferret
4 Monarch
5 Blue whale
6 Mountain tapir
7 Spectacled bear
8 Amazon river dolphin
9 Hyacinth macaw
10 Golden lion tamarin
11 Maned wolf
12 Atlantic puffin
13 Southwestern water vole
14 Western spadefoot toad
15 Hermann's tortoise
16 European bison
17 Mediterranean monk seal
18 West African giraffe
19 Sawfish
20 Dwarf crocodile
21 Western lowland gorilla
22 Ethiopian wolf

23 Black-and-white ruffed lemur
24 Asian elephant
25 Bactrian camel
26 Takin
27 Red panda
28 Siberian tiger
29 Japanese crane
30 Great hammerhead
31 Coral
32 Tree kangaroo
33 New Caledonia flying fox
34 Komodo dragon

Endangered animals
around the world

The Atlantic puffin

During the mating season, the Atlantic puffin's colorful beak and feet help attract mates.

Standing on its tiny bright orange feet, its plump white belly pushed forward, a strange bird busies itself in front of its burrow. The bright red stripes on its beak and the black line over its eyes make it look almost like a clown.

It is the mating season, and the Atlantic puffin is looking for materials to make its nest. Collecting feathers, grass, and moss, it bravely roams cliffs swept by freezing winds. This high seas bird spends most of its time alone, returning to the coast only to reproduce in huge colonies as noisy as they are colorful. Its behavior becomes particularly interesting after mating: The Atlantic puffin digs a hole to protect its offspring, just like the rabbit. The male puffin is primarily responsible for this task. With light taps of its beak and feet, it can dig a tunnel 3 to 6 feet long.

When the chick hatches, the couple takes turns fishing and feeding it small fish. Puffins may be a little clumsy and look like clowns on land, but they are masters in the water. Their fishing technique is unbeatable: They can dive as deep as 200 feet, swimming with their short wings and directing themselves with their feet. In order to bring back as much food as possible, they store their catch between their tongue and upper jaw. It isn't unusual for an adult to return from fishing with thirty fish hanging from both sides of its beak.

The Atlantic puffin catches small fish to feed its young.

A funny bird

This funny bird digs a hole in which to build a nest where it will raise its young.

Atlantic puffins live in the north of the Atlantic Ocean and in Europe, as well as in Asia and North Africa!

Though it is still frequently seen in the north of the Atlantic Ocean, the Atlantic puffin is extremely threatened in Europe. Its numbers dropped considerably at the beginning of the last century due to hunting and poaching. Currently, it is still prey to many dangers, such as hydrocarbon pollution and the gradual diminishing of its food sources due to climate change.

Young Atlantic puffins are also particularly sensitive to the lights we turn on when night falls. When they start to fly, many puffins are drawn to city lights instead of to the open sea and are unable to find their way back. Many species of birds living along coastlines are victims of this problem, as are migratory birds, some of which travel at night. They often collide with illuminated buildings. This light pollution is a nuisance not only to birds, but to insects and plants, which can no longer tell night from day. By turning off a few unnecessary lights, we could make a big impact while saving power at the same time!

◀ It appears that the colors of the Atlantic puffin's feathers serve as camouflage. The white of its belly makes it less visible to predators from the depths of the sea, and the black of its back is difficult for flying predators to spot.

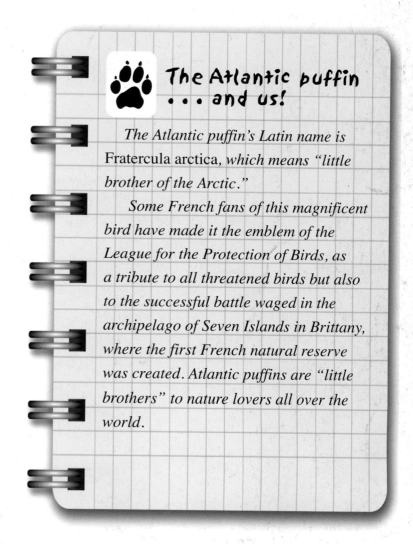

The Atlantic puffin ... and us!

The Atlantic puffin's Latin name is Fratercula arctica, *which means "little brother of the Arctic."*

Some French fans of this magnificent bird have made it the emblem of the League for the Protection of Birds, as a tribute to all threatened birds but also to the successful battle waged in the archipelago of Seven Islands in Brittany, where the first French natural reserve was created. Atlantic puffins are "little brothers" to nature lovers all over the world.

The Southwestern water vole

Unlike most rodents, the Southwestern water vole is diurnal.
This means it is active during the day and rests at night.

T hough it is also called a "water rat," the Southwestern water vole is not a rat at all! With its round little face, tiny ears, silky coat, and endearing expressions, it is an adorable rodent. It is only found in France, Spain, and Portugal.

The Southwestern water vole shows no real adaptation to aquatic life (it doesn't even have webbed feet), yet it cannot do without water. In fact, its entire life depends on it. Therefore, it's found near calm rivers, lakes, and swampy areas. In winter and in summer, it spends all day bustling about on the shore. Sometimes it gnaws on aquatic plants; sometimes it feasts on rushes, reeds, or grasses. You might even catch it eating some insects or small amphibians. And when it feels like taking a dip in the water, it becomes a formidable swimmer, able to remain underwater for minutes at a time. Even its shelter is dug into the bank. It makes its nest at the end of a tunnel that often begins with a stockroom where it piles up pieces of grass. The Southwestern water vole digs two openings to its burrow: one leading out to the open air and another that leads underwater.

For shelter, the Southwestern water vole digs a hole in the bank.

Don't mistake it for a rat!

If you leave a corner of your garden wild, it can become home to an entire family of fauna, some of which are threatened, like the Southwestern water vole.

The Southwestern water vole is found in France, Spain, and Portugal.

The number of these once-common little rodents is dropping rapidly, to the point that they have entirely vanished from certain areas. Since its diet essentially consists of wild plants, the Southwestern water vole is completely harmless to human agricultural activities. But it is often confused with other rodents such as the nutria or the rat and falls victim to rat eradication campaigns.

Yet the main threat to the water vole is the transformation of its environment. By modifying watercourses to irrigate fields, lining riverbanks with stones, or varying water levels, we are gradually reducing its habitat. Additionally, the rare places where this little rodent could establish itself are often occupied by invasive foreign species such as the nutria or the muskrat, which are bigger and more numerous.

The Southwestern water vole is not the only species facing these kinds of problems: Our modification of many natural habitats is the leading cause of extinction!

◄ Even if you can't see the Southwestern water vole, you can observe signs of its presence: the "dining rooms" recognizable by areas covered in leftovers of a meal (beveled grass) and the "restrooms" formed for the animal's waste.

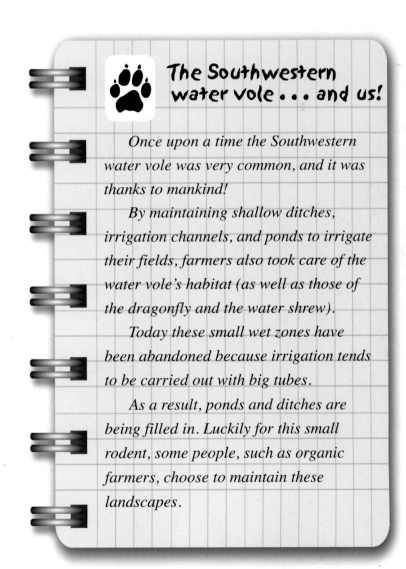

The Southwestern water vole . . . and us!

Once upon a time the Southwestern water vole was very common, and it was thanks to mankind!

By maintaining shallow ditches, irrigation channels, and ponds to irrigate their fields, farmers also took care of the water vole's habitat (as well as those of the dragonfly and the water shrew).

Today these small wet zones have been abandoned because irrigation tends to be carried out with big tubes.

As a result, ponds and ditches are being filled in. Luckily for this small rodent, some people, such as organic farmers, choose to maintain these landscapes.

The Western spadefoot toad

The Western spadefood toad primarily eats invertebrates. It takes advantage of the darkness of night to go in search of spiders, butterflies, dragonflies, and insect larvae.

Unlike its fellow toads, the Western spadefoot toad's smooth skin does not have any warts, and its pupils form a vertical slit like those of a cat, which gives it a friendly sort of look.

It can only be found in three European countries: France, Spain, and Portugal. But it is not widespread. This amphibian is highly sensitive to its environment: It needs open, loose-soiled ground, such as sand dunes, situated near a watering hole. The loose soil helps when it digs its deep burrows. It can dig down as far as 3 feet! To pull this off, it uses small projections on its hind legs, which are known as "spades." This is why we call it the Western spadefoot toad. It cannot live without its shelter, for it spends an enormous amount of time there and only goes out on rainy nights.

Yet toward the end of winter, the male finally ventures out of its hiding place to dive into the closest pond and "sing" to attract females. In fact, its "song" is more like a funny clucking that sounds a lot like a hen's. After reproducing, females lay their eggs in long ribbons, wrapping them around aquatic plants. A few days later, surprisingly long tadpoles will emerge from these eggs: 7 inches . . . longer than a regular mailing envelope!

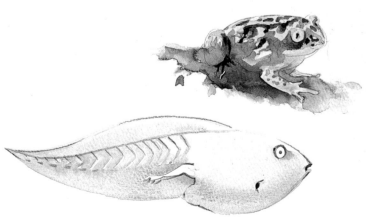

The Western spadefoot toad tadpole is nearly twice the size of an adult.

An unusual toad

Humid zones (like lakes, swamps, and mangroves) are vanishing. Yet they are full of rich biodiversity.

The Western spadefood toad lives in Spain, Portugal, and the South and Southwest of France.

One in three amphibians is threatened with extinction. The Western spadefoot toad is among those in danger. For several years, it has been a victim of the destruction of its habitat due to the growth of cities and the spread of intensive agriculture. This strange toad lives near ponds along the seashore, of which it is particularly fond. Unfortunately, these areas are severely abused by people.

In order to get rid of mosquitoes or construct seaside homes, we fill in watering holes, leaving the spadefoot toad without places to lay its eggs.

In 1992, the European Union created the "Natura 2000," an ecological network of protected areas where species such as the Western spadefoot toad cannot be disturbed. These are environmentally crucial zones where animal and plant species are preserved in an effort to reconcile their protection with human activities.

◀ The Western spadefoot toad is a funny toad. While its squat appearance is similar to that of its fellow toads, its smooth skin and vertical pupils clearly distinguish it from the others.

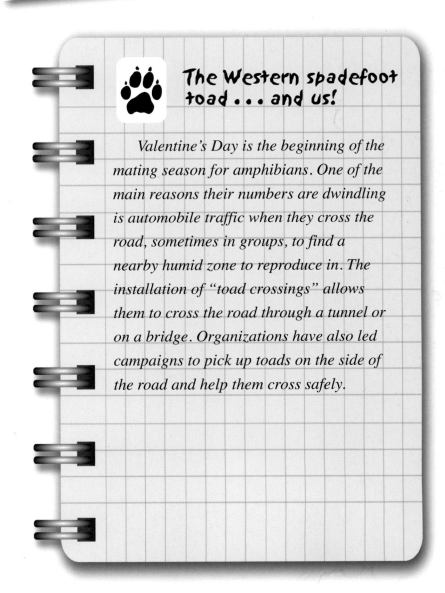

The Western spadefoot toad... and us!

Valentine's Day is the beginning of the mating season for amphibians. One of the main reasons their numbers are dwindling is automobile traffic when they cross the road, sometimes in groups, to find a nearby humid zone to reproduce in. The installation of "toad crossings" allows them to cross the road through a tunnel or on a bridge. Organizations have also led campaigns to pick up toads on the side of the road and help them cross safely.

Hermann's tortoise

Like all reptiles, Hermann's tortoises are cold-blooded animals, which means that their body temperature varies according to the temperature outside. This is why they stretch out in the morning sun to warm up.

Hermann's tortoises are small- to medium-size tortoises that come from southern Europe, and can even be found on the shores of the Mediterranean.

These tortoises depend on the right temperatures for many reasons, including breeding. After coupling, the female is able to keep the male's seed inside her for up to four full years if the conditions in her habitat are not suitable for her offspring. Only when the situation is favorable will her eggs develop and be laid.

Another very curious thing takes place after the laying of eggs: The baby turtles' sexes will be determined by the ground temperature. When the temperature is greater than 86°F, the young will be born female, but if the temperature is lower than 82°F, they will all be males!

After three months, the young come out of the ground. Though they are no bigger than a couple of sugar cubes, the little turtles are now able to take care of themselves. But because their shells are still soft, they have no real protection from predators.

The female Hermann's tortoise digs a hole in which to lay her eggs with her hind legs.

A surprising reptile

An unattended fire, a barbecue, a cigarette butt, or a piece of glass focusing sunbeams can start a forest fire, which threaten animals' habitats.

The Hermann's tortoise can be found in Europe, on the shores of the Mediterranean from France to Turkey.

The Hermann's tortoise does not claim a very extensive territory. It is only found in Europe, on the shores of the Mediterranean from France to Turkey. A victim of its popularity, it has too often been removed from its natural habitat to be sold or placed in gardens. Nowadays, despite a law that strictly forbids capturing a Hermann's tortoise, people continue to do so, and they are becoming increasingly rare in the wild.

Additionally, the few Hermann's tortoises that have survived in the Mediterranean scrubland are having increasing trouble finding their place. With the expansion of cities and agriculture, they have extreme difficulty locating quiet spots to live in. The forests they inhabit must be protected, particularly now that climate change favors drought and the propagation of fires. Fires, which are often started by people, are a devastating threat to the defenseless Hermann's tortoise.

◄ Just like a fledgling, this young Hermann's tortoise uses its "egg tooth," a small spike near the tip of its beak, to break out of its shell.

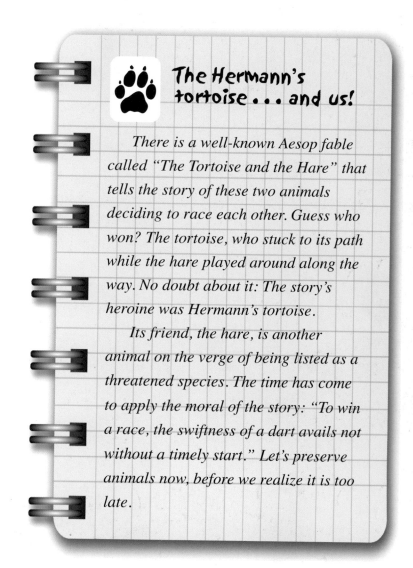

The Hermann's tortoise... and us!

There is a well-known Aesop fable called "The Tortoise and the Hare" that tells the story of these two animals deciding to race each other. Guess who won? The tortoise, who stuck to its path while the hare played around along the way. No doubt about it: The story's heroine was Hermann's tortoise.

Its friend, the hare, is another animal on the verge of being listed as a threatened species. The time has come to apply the moral of the story: "To win a race, the swiftness of a dart avails not without a timely start." Let's preserve animals now, before we realize it is too late.

The Mediterranean monk seal

Stretching about 10 feet and weighing nearly 1,000 pounds, the Mediterranean monk seal is the biggest seal in the world.

The monk seal is a marine mammal, like dolphins and whales, living in the warm waters of the Mediterranean.

With big, dark eyes, a round and endearing little face, fur like velvet . . . the monk seal is a real beauty.

Its admirably tapered body, small flipper-shaped limbs, underwater vision, and watertight nostrils for diving also make it an incredible swimmer.

The monk seal cannot stay underwater for very long (no more than six minutes), but it has become a champion at concealing itself. And this explains why we don't know much about its behavior. The invasion of beaches by hordes of noisy tourists totally changed this shy animal's habits before we had a chance to study them.

The monk seal used to live in large colonies on deserted sunny beaches, but it has been forced to take refuge in places inaccessible to people. Females have even begun giving birth in caves with underwater entrances.

Formerly, the monk seal lived in large colonies on deserted beaches. Nowadays, they take refuge in underwater caves to get away from human activity.

A shy seal

The coasts of the Mediterranean are increasingly busy as tourist numbers rise, leaving seals at a loss for space.

The monk seal lives along the shores of the Mediterranean, though it is increasingly rare to see it there.

With a total population of no more than 450 individuals, the monk seal is one of the six most threatened marine mammal species in the world. It was once found all along the shores of the Mediterranean. Today it is very rare to see one.

The list of threats hanging over the monk seal is a long one. Many seals are harmed by water pollution or the decrease in food due to excessive fishing. Some get caught in fishing nets and drown, while others are killed by fishermen.

But the most serious issue at the moment is our expanding presence along the seashore. This seal is so shy that it would rather move elsewhere than share space with humans. The only problem is that wild areas have become extremely rare, not only in the Mediterranean but in the majority of coastal areas. The need to create protected zones along the seashore is an urgent one.

◀ Two traits distinguish the Mediterranean monk seal from other seals. Unlike its kin in the frozen oceans, the Mediterranean seal has short fur for warm waters, and males and pups have a characteristic white spot near their belly buttons.

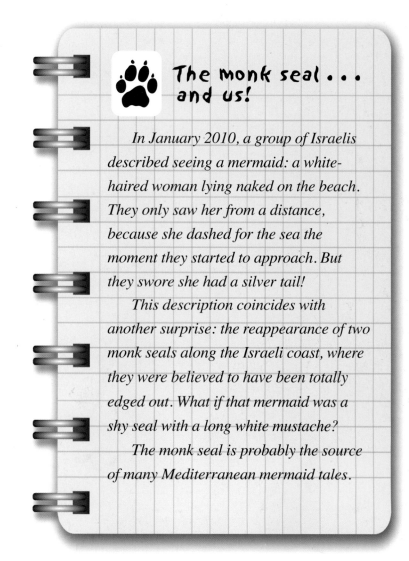

The monk seal... and us!

In January 2010, a group of Israelis described seeing a mermaid: a white-haired woman lying naked on the beach. They only saw her from a distance, because she dashed for the sea the moment they started to approach. But they swore she had a silver tail!

This description coincides with another surprise: the reappearance of two monk seals along the Israeli coast, where they were believed to have been totally edged out. What if that mermaid was a shy seal with a long white mustache?

The monk seal is probably the source of many Mediterranean mermaid tales.

The European bison

Dominance among European bison is essentially established during the mating season. The bison that wins these battles, the strongest and often the oldest of the herd, will mate with the females.

No joke: There really are bison in Europe! In fact, these giants are the largest land mammals found on the continent (largely in Eastern Europe). This bison is different from its American cousin, but what sets them apart?

At first glance, it's their silhouettes. The European bovine is more slender than the American. Standing an impressive 6½ feet at the shoulder and weighing up to 2,650 pounds, the European bison appears less stocky. Unlike the American bison, whose coat is particularly thick on the head and shoulders, that of the European bison is equally distributed over its whole body, which reinforces the impression of its large size.

They also display slightly different behaviors. We can all picture the gigantic herds populating the vast plains of the American West. This is far from the case in Europe, where European bison live in the forest. This is probably why their horns, which are longer than the American bison's, are set closer together. They need to get through the trees, after all!

The European bison is an impressive animal: It is nearly 6½ feet tall at the shoulder.

The colossus of the woods

The American bison is stockier than its European kin.

The European bison now lives in Eastern Europe, in protected areas.

The history of the European bison is a real adventure, for it nearly vanished in the 1920s. There was a time when it was very common, found from the Atlantic Ocean to Russia. Although the bison was exterminated by intensive hunting and the destruction of forests, a few individuals survived in a handful of zoos.

Thanks to programs dedicated to having the animals reproduce in captivity, their numbers grew, and beginning in the 1950s, they were reintroduced into nature.

Despite difficult beginnings, these herbivores released from captivity adapted well to life in the wild: It is estimated there are about 2,000 of them now living in protected natural habitats.

These 2,000 wild bison are descended from only twelve individuals! In other words, they are all related. The downside to this, as often happens when individuals of the same family are coupled, is that there are some health issues among their offspring, including bone and fertility problems.

◀ The European bison lives in familial herds. When it is threatened, it opts for intimidation: Swinging its enormous head, it tensely scratches at the ground and eventually charges!

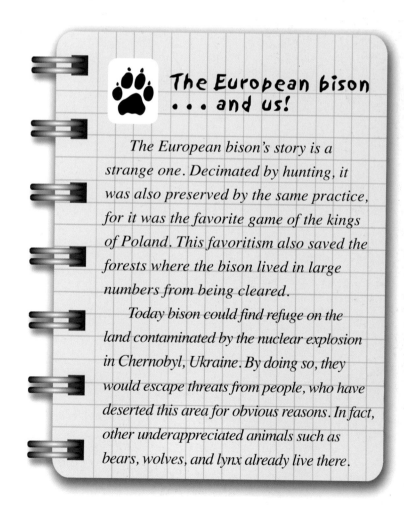

The European bison . . . and us!

The European bison's story is a strange one. Decimated by hunting, it was also preserved by the same practice, for it was the favorite game of the kings of Poland. This favoritism also saved the forests where the bison lived in large numbers from being cleared.

Today bison could find refuge on the land contaminated by the nuclear explosion in Chernobyl, Ukraine. By doing so, they would escape threats from people, who have deserted this area for obvious reasons. In fact, other underappreciated animals such as bears, wolves, and lynx already live there.

The Asian elephant

Elephants communicate with each other through caresses and growls. Some of these sounds are transmitted through the ground and can be perceived by fellow elephants at a radius of one mile!

The colossal Asian elephant lives under the trees of the Southeast Asian rain forest in crushing mugginess, surrounded by the rustling of a multitude of insects and the powerful cries of acrobatic monkeys. Yet it does not hold the record for the largest land animal. Weighing a maximum of five tons (about the weight of three cars), it doesn't measure up to the African elephant, which can weigh up to seven tons. Nonetheless, it has a phenomenal appetite, gulping down about 330 pounds of leaves and 25 gallons of water a day!

The elephant's most formidable characteristic is its trunk. This multipurpose organ serves as a nose, a hand, an arm, a watering can, and a club. Weighing more than 220 pounds (heavier than most grown men!) and consisting of more than 100,000 muscles, the elephant's trunk has incredible power. It can lift up to 660 pounds!

Unfortunately, the elephant's prodigious strength, intelligence, and docile character have led to it be exploited by people for more than 5,000 years.

The elephant's strength is heavily exploited by humans.

Daily assistance

Asian elephants
are not domestic animals. Yet in some
places they have accompanied humans
for centuries.

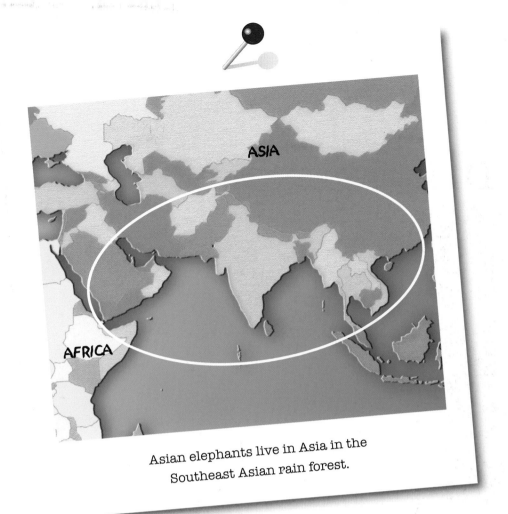

Asian elephants live in Asia in the
Southeast Asian rain forest.

Cleared for its wood or to be turned into farmland, the Asian rain forest has been reduced to a few scraps. Yet Asia's biggest mammal needs the forests to live in. The Asian elephant is therefore becoming increasingly rare in the wild. And as if that weren't enough, those still surviving in freedom are threatened by poaching. Their tusks are sought after for their ivory. Unlike African elephants, where both sexes are tusked, only the male Asian elephant has tusks. Poachers therefore largely kill males, to the point that in some areas there is only one male to every hundred females, making it extremely difficult for herds to maintain their size and genetic diversity.

Over the last few years, elephant poaching has been on the rise around the world. Regulations in certain countries such as Thailand are not strict enough to limit this kind of illegal trade, and ivory still winds up on markets as decorative objects.

Tourists should avoid buying anything made of ivory. They could risk becoming a trafficker without even realizing it.

◀ From an early age, the elephant is taught to submit to human commands by a trainer known as a "mahout" so that it will carry loads on its back or move tree trunks on plantations.

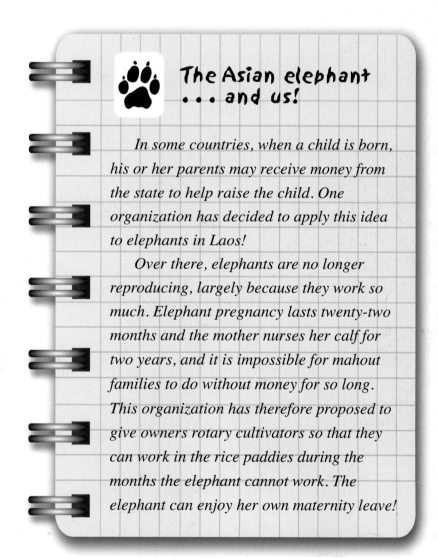

🐾 The Asian elephant ... and us!

In some countries, when a child is born, his or her parents may receive money from the state to help raise the child. One organization has decided to apply this idea to elephants in Laos!

Over there, elephants are no longer reproducing, largely because they work so much. Elephant pregnancy lasts twenty-two months and the mother nurses her calf for two years, and it is impossible for mahout families to do without money for so long. This organization has therefore proposed to give owners rotary cultivators so that they can work in the rice paddies during the months the elephant cannot work. The elephant can enjoy her own maternity leave!

The Bactrian camel

Domesticated for nearly 5,000 years, the Bactrian camel is still used as a pack animal and is bred for its wool, milk, and meat. About 1.4 million Bactrian camels are alive and domesticated today. Only around 800 remain in the wild.

To avoid any confusion, let's review the two types of camels. One type of camel has two humps and lives in Asia, while the other, the dromedary, only has one hump and can be found in North Africa. Nonetheless, both make the same sound: They bray.

Just like its African cousin, the Bactrian camel is incredibly well adapted to the extreme living conditions found in deserts. In these areas of central Asia, water is extremely rare, and temperatures can drop as low as -40°F in winter and rise to 104°F in summer. Only exceptional creatures can survive this kind of temperature variation.

The camel has several characteristics allowing it to store up and avoid wasting water, but the most ingenious system is in its humps, which accumulate fat.

During difficult times, this fat turns into energy or water. Thanks to this subtle trick, the camel can go eight days without drinking! Additionally, in order to withstand extreme temperatures, it has developed a waterproof woolly fleece, which is 4 inches thick, can weigh up to 33 pounds, and is a perfect insulator.

The camel is
one of the mammals
best adapted to extreme climates.

The ship of the desert

The lives of camels and Asian nomads are closely linked: The camel's wool, milk, and strength are essential for maintaining the nomad's lifestyle.

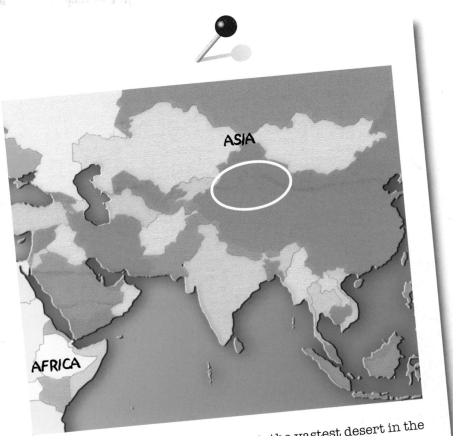

The animal lives in the Gobi Desert, the vastest desert in the world, between northern China and southern Mongolia.

The Bactrian camel is in a worrisome situation. Only about one thousand remain in the wild. These camels are now only found in a single place on earth, in the world's largest desert: the Gobi Desert.

They are threatened with extinction because they have long been hunted for meat. Additionally, the desert is growing at a disturbingly fast rate due to deforestation and the expansion of pastures. Their habitat is also threatened by illegal mining operations and the laying of gas pipelines. Bit by bit, the rare watering holes where the camels were accustomed to finding water are disappearing.

The camel's future is made all the more fragile by the fact that scientists have recently noticed that domesticated camels cannot be reintroduced into their natural habitat. Indeed, those that have been domesticated for several thousands of years have evolved separately from those in the wild; they no longer have exactly the same genes. They would be at risk of not adapting to truly extreme conditions. It is very difficult and sometimes dangerous to reintroduce these animals to a natural habitat: This is why it is better to protect the wild animals still found there. Their mere presence also allows for the preservation of a balanced ecosystem.

◄ The Bactrian camel's wool is of a particularly high quality. It is sought after because it is among the finest, softest, and most insulating wools.

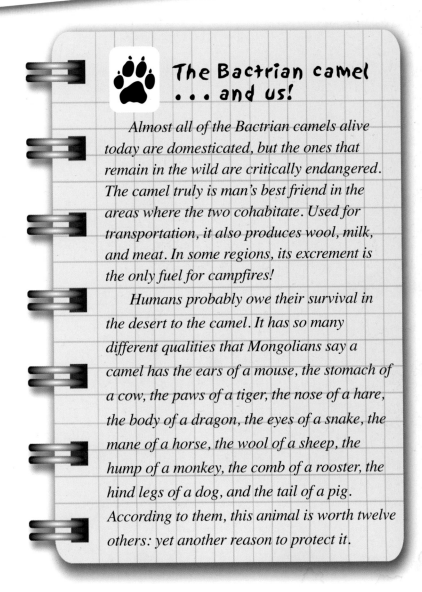

🐾 The Bactrian camel ... and us!

Almost all of the Bactrian camels alive today are domesticated, but the ones that remain in the wild are critically endangered. The camel truly is man's best friend in the areas where the two cohabitate. Used for transportation, it also produces wool, milk, and meat. In some regions, its excrement is the only fuel for campfires!

Humans probably owe their survival in the desert to the camel. It has so many different qualities that Mongolians say a camel has the ears of a mouse, the stomach of a cow, the paws of a tiger, the nose of a hare, the body of a dragon, the eyes of a snake, the mane of a horse, the wool of a sheep, the hump of a monkey, the comb of a rooster, the hind legs of a dog, and the tail of a pig. According to them, this animal is worth twelve others: yet another reason to protect it.

The takin

The takin is an herbivore that feeds on leaves, grasses, and young shoots. It is also a great consumer of salt, which it finds by licking rocks.

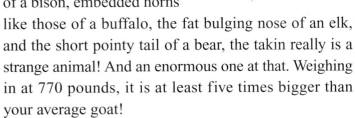

The takin is a zoo all to itself! With the massive body of a cow, the powerful neck of a bison, embedded horns like those of a buffalo, the fat bulging nose of an elk, and the short pointy tail of a bear, the takin really is a strange animal! And an enormous one at that. Weighing in at 770 pounds, it is at least five times bigger than your average goat!

The takin is little known because it is extremely fearful and lives hidden on the slopes of the highest mountain chain in the world: the Himalayas. It can be found at altitudes between 3,000 and 15,000 feet, and that's really high! (Mount McKinley, the highest peak in North America, is 20,320 feet tall.) Living so high up, the takin needs to be able to ward off cold and humidity.

Its long and dense coat of fur and thick layer of fat are fine assets. But the most surprising adaptation is that it has glands that secrete an oily liquid that spreads over its fur to make it totally waterproof—a real ski jacket! And that's not all. Its strange bulging nose contains large cavities (its sinuses) that allow it to warm cold air before it takes the air into its lungs. Without that, the takin would be frozen in no time at all.

Due to the peculiar color of its coat, the takin is believed to be the source of the legend of the Golden Fleece.

The Golden Fleece

The forests of the Himalayan mountains shelter and feed many animals. They are also vital sources of necessities for local populations.

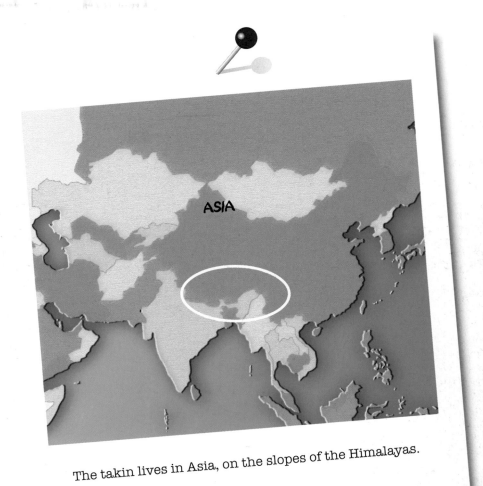

The takin lives in Asia, on the slopes of the Himalayas.

According to the International Union for Conservation of Nature, one mammal in five is threatened with extinction. This is true of the takin. It lives in inaccessible areas, which makes it difficult to assess the number of individuals currently remaining. Yet we know that their numbers have dropped significantly in the last twenty years. Though protective measures have been put in place in certain countries, this superb herbivore continues to be hunted for its meat and its highly sought-after shaded-tone fleece. Still, deforestation remains the most significant threat to the takin.

On some slopes of the Himalayas, forests have been so exploited that the entire landscape looks like the moon. They have been cleared by the extraction of firewood as well as mined resources such as gold, copper, or uranium, or for use as farmland.

This area, one of the richest in fauna and flora, is facing irreversible losses. Local communities must commit themselves to the management of their area's resources in order to avoid degrading them but also to ensure they do not become victims of this exploitation as well.

◀ The takin lives in wooded zones in mountains and high-altitude prairies, where it migrates during the warm season.

The takin... and us!

A long, long time ago (more than 3,000 years ago!), the Greeks wrote legendary tales whose heroes included Hercules, Odysseus, and Jason, and they have remained famous to this day. Jason was a prince who could claim his throne only by bringing home the Golden Fleece, which ensured prosperity to a distant country. This fleece was probably the takin's splendid golden fur.

We do not know how true the story is, but this extraordinary animal will certainly continue to inspire fabulous tales for many more millennia if we take the trouble to protect it now.

The Japanese crane

Japanese cranes gather in large numbers
on the banks of marshes.

W hat could be more graceful than this long young lady, whose height of 5 feet and wingspan of almost 8 feet make her one of the biggest birds in the world?

Surrounded by a thick coat of snow, a couple of Japanese cranes prepare to court, and when they are finished, they will stay together for life. Their plumage of immaculate white, with the exception of the black on their necks and at the tips of their wings, gives them a delicate, light appearance. To finish off the picture, their skin forms an elegant bright red cap at the top of their skull. Japanese cranes gradually grow closer over the course of their spectacular nuptial displays. Arching their long necks with a trumpeting call, their immense wings outstretched, they execute large leaps, rising like feathers in the wind.

Found in southeastern Asia, including China and Japan, they depend on water, building their nests in the reeds and feeding on aquatic organisms. Their long pointy beaks can harpoon anything they can reach: fish, amphibians, insects, and mollusks, as well as grass. In other words, they are omnivores . . . just like people!

During the nuptial display, cranes perform a beautiful ballet.

53

An elegant dancer

Throughout the world, animals represent meaningful human values: For instance, the Japanese crane symbolizes hope and love.

The Japanese crane lives in humid zones in southeastern Asia.

Japanese cranes narrowly escaped extinction. The humid zones in which they live (swamps, rivers, lakes) were severely mistreated by humans. Drained for construction or for turning into fields, these areas rich in fauna and flora are becoming rare. Today, it is believed that wild habitats support only 2,750 Japanese cranes.

Yet the future of this great bird does not appear so bleak. Many organizations around the world have rallied to save it, helping to raise awareness among locals, create reserves, or reintroduce the bird. Eggs laid by captive cranes are sent to sanctuaries and then artificially incubated.

After hatching, the young are raised in groups, without direct contact with people, so they can retain their wild nature. Finally, when the fledglings are able to take care of themselves, they are set free in a reserve. And it works! Since these projects were initiated, the number of Japanese cranes has gradually increased.

◀ A symbol of love and faithfulness in the Land of the Rising Sun, Japanese crane couples stay together for life.

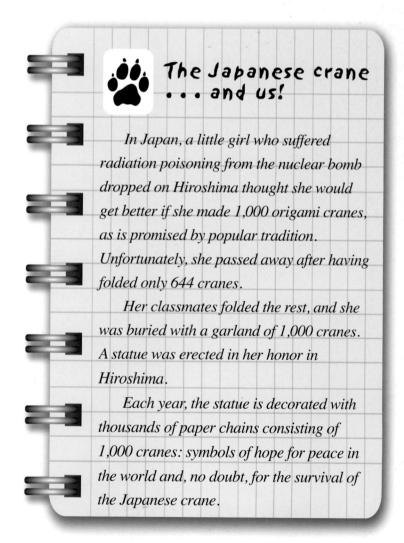

The Japanese crane ... and us!

In Japan, a little girl who suffered radiation poisoning from the nuclear bomb dropped on Hiroshima thought she would get better if she made 1,000 origami cranes, as is promised by popular tradition. Unfortunately, she passed away after having folded only 644 cranes.

Her classmates folded the rest, and she was buried with a garland of 1,000 cranes. A statue was erected in her honor in Hiroshima.

Each year, the statue is decorated with thousands of paper chains consisting of 1,000 cranes: symbols of hope for peace in the world and, no doubt, for the survival of the Japanese crane.

The Siberian tiger

During winter, the Siberian tiger's fur thickens to allow it to survive in the freezing cold.

Of all felines, the Siberian tiger is by far the most imposing and, with some males reaching close to 700 pounds, easily the heaviest! It is undoubtedly a most formidable predator.

It will not eat sick animals or feed on dead ones; instead, it attacks very large prey such as buffalo, deer, elk, and boars. Its hunting method consists of getting as close as possible to its target before the attack. Its vertically striped fur allows it to blend in with the forest's pattern of shadow and light. And in winter, its coat brightens so it can hide in the snow.

A nocturnal hunter, it has exceptional night vision that is six times more acute than a person's. Once it has spotted its prey, it leaps onto it with phenomenal strength and grabs hold of the nape of its neck.

With its 2¾-inch canines and its powerful jaws that can easily crush bone, the tiger is able to rapidly overcome its victim.

When the snow carpets the forest, the tiger's coat becomes a lighter color so it can blend in as it hunts down its prey.

A large predator

In order to help tigers, try using recycled paper and avoid products that contain palm oil, which can contribute to the destruction of the tiger's habitat. Also try eating organic and/or local products.

This animal can be found in the coniferous forest of Siberia.

Like other large land predators, the Siberian tiger is currently endangered. Only approximately 400 individuals remain in the wild, with about as many in captivity.

Originally, there were far more tigers, but they have been decimated by intensive poaching. The power and beauty of the Siberian tiger make it a highly sought-after animal on Asian markets. People pay a fortune for every part of its body: its splendid fur; its bones, teeth, claws; and even its organs, which are alleged to have healing powers.

Like many other animals, the tiger is a victim of deforestation. The coniferous forest where it lives has recently become coveted by timber companies, which export wood to make furniture, construction materials, and paper.

Learning how to benefit from forests in environmentally friendly ways and recycling paper could well be among the solutions for saving this splendid feline.

◀ Like most wildcats, young tigers spend much of their time playing. These sparring matches simulating combat allow them to develop their muscles and practice hunting.

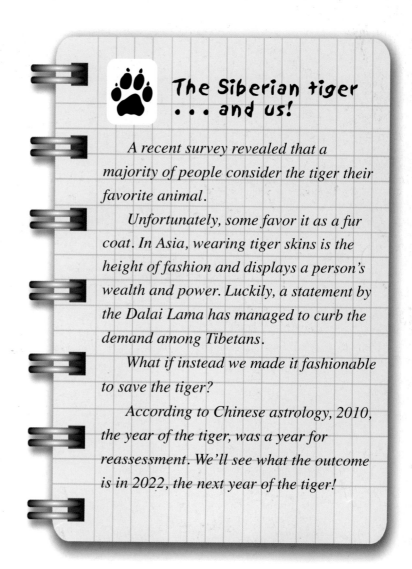

The Siberian tiger ... and us!

A recent survey revealed that a majority of people consider the tiger their favorite animal.

Unfortunately, some favor it as a fur coat. In Asia, wearing tiger skins is the height of fashion and displays a person's wealth and power. Luckily, a statement by the Dalai Lama has managed to curb the demand among Tibetans.

What if instead we made it fashionable to save the tiger?

According to Chinese astrology, 2010, the year of the tiger, was a year for reassessment. We'll see what the outcome is in 2022, the next year of the tiger!

The red panda

The red panda is tremendously well adapted to life in the high mountains. To combat extreme cold, every part of its body is covered in thick fur . . . with the exception of the tip of its nose!

Let's set things straight: The real panda is the red panda. This small animal—no bigger than a fox— was discovered before the giant panda.

Although the red panda and the giant panda share many characteristics, they are two different animals. The black-and-white panda is a bear, while the red panda is the only representative of its own family.

Since they live in the same forests, where bamboo grows under tall trees, these two animals have evolved in similar ways over time. They share the peculiar trait of eating bamboo nearly exclusively, which is rather surprising for animals whose digestive systems are that of a carnivore.

In order to take hold of bamboo shoots, red pandas have developed a bone on the side of their paws that acts like a fake thumb. It allows them to easily manipulate bamboo branches. This bone is indispensable, as pandas spend more than eight hours a day feasting on their favorite food.

In order to take hold of bamboo branches, the red panda uses a "thumb" on its forepaws.

An adorable mammal

The exploitation of forests is not always harmful when it is managed with respect for biodiversity and the humans who live in them.

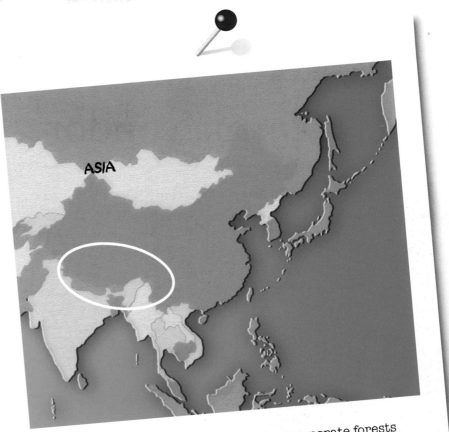

The red panda lives in Asia, in the temperate forests of the foothills of the Himalayas.

The red panda lives in the temperate forests of the foothills of the Himalayas. It might seem that this mammal would easily find habitats that suit it in this vast mountain chain stretching across Asia. Far from it. The red panda is not common at all. In fact, it is becoming increasingly rare as the size of red panda populations gradually diminishes.

As with most endangered species, there are several reasons for the red panda's decline, but the principal one is the destruction of its environment. Its forests are used for firewood, cut down for the timber industry, and divided up by fields and roads, all of which makes them hostile, uninhabitable environments for the panda. In some countries, the red panda is also poached for its fur, which is used to make hats.

Fur trafficking is a threat to many other species, including the panther, the otter, and the seal. Some species have even come close to totally vanishing just because of the demand for their furs.

◀ Like a cat or a bear, the red panda has the digestive system of a carnivore. Yet its diet is mostly herbivorous: It eats bamboo nearly exclusively.

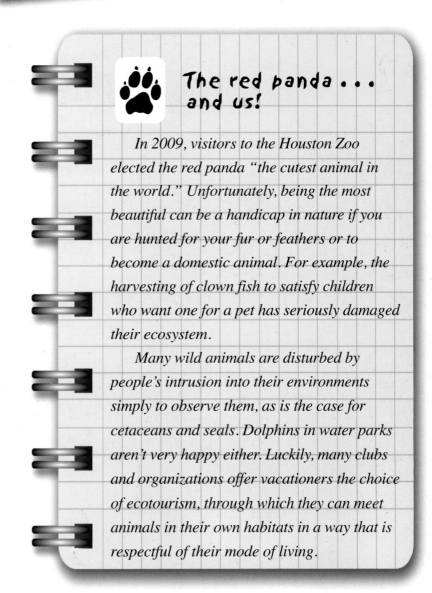

The red panda . . . and us!

In 2009, visitors to the Houston Zoo elected the red panda "the cutest animal in the world." Unfortunately, being the most beautiful can be a handicap in nature if you are hunted for your fur or feathers or to become a domestic animal. For example, the harvesting of clown fish to satisfy children who want one for a pet has seriously damaged their ecosystem.

Many wild animals are disturbed by people's intrusion into their environments simply to observe them, as is the case for cetaceans and seals. Dolphins in water parks aren't very happy either. Luckily, many clubs and organizations offer vacationers the choice of ecotourism, through which they can meet animals in their own habitats in a way that is respectful of their mode of living.

The California condor

Outlined with a ruffle of fine black feathers, the head and neck of the California condor are covered in red-orange skin.

It is one of the biggest birds in the world. When fully extended, its wings span up to 9.8 feet. That's huge! (It is about the size of two children, with one standing on the other's head!) The condor's wingspan allows it to be carried by the breeze with only a rare flap of its wings. Thanks to its ability to glide, it can cover great distances each day to find its food.

This vulture is very important to the environment it inhabits: It plays the role of nature's cleaner by feeding on dead animals. Contrary to popular belief, it is not a dirty animal, but of course, it is a messy eater.

When it feeds, the condor plunges its head into carcasses and feasts, which may explain why it's bald. Without feathers, the pieces of meat stuck to its skin fall off more easily as they dry. After a meal, the condor takes time to clean up a little. It rubs its head and neck on the grass or against the rocks and spends several hours smoothing its feathers.

As soon as it can, it bathes or stands in the rain in order to properly rinse its plumage. Then it spreads its wings out in the wind to let them dry.

When it spreads its wings, the California condor is one of the biggest birds in the world.

A powerful glider

Waste often winds up in nature, although it may not always be visible. Heavy metals from batteries and lead shot, toxic products from detergents, and pesticides can end up polluting rivers.

NORTH AMERICA

Today the California condor glides over the wild areas of the Pacific Coast again.

Once upon a time the California condor glided in the sky over all of North America. Hunting, poisoning, and the collection of eggs by people have led it to the verge of extinction. By 1987, the rare survivors could only be found in captivity. A few years later, though, the young born in captivity were reintroduced in the remaining wild areas of the Pacific Coast. And this initiative has proved quite helpful: More than 130 individuals have recently been counted.

Unfortunately, researchers also observed that these birds were suffering from a very serious illness due to their massive consumption of lead: saturnism, or lead poisoning. When vultures eat carcasses of animals killed or wounded by hunters, they also swallow the lead shot still inside them.

Left in the wild, lead shot contaminates the entire environment and many other animals, not just the condor. This is why major public awareness campaigns have been organized to reach hunters and encourage them to use less toxic munitions and to hunt in a responsible manner.

◄ California condors' wings are sometimes equipped with electronic tags that allow us to track their movements in order to better protect them. Even with the tags, they can fly at speeds of more than 50 mph.

The California condor... and us!

Just like the California condor, humans could be considered one of the most contaminated species in the world! Heavy metals, pesticides, and chemical products are all over the planet. Water carries the pollutants it encounters to the sea, spreading these substances in all natural environments, including plants. Small fish feed on them. A bigger fish will eat them, accumulating all their pollutants. This growing contamination also reaches cetaceans, people, and the condor, which is at the very end of the food chain that links us all. Our future and that of biodiversity are inextricably connected.

The blue whale

The blue whale produces high-intensity but low-frequency sounds that allow it to communicate with fellow whales up to hundreds of miles away.

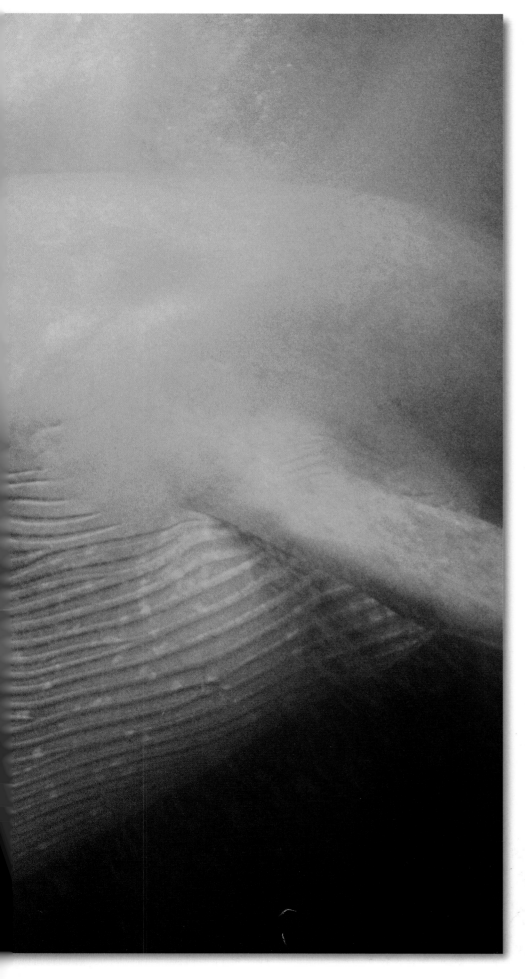

Gigantic is an appropriate description of the blue whale. It is the biggest animal that has ever lived on our planet.

Even the most imposing dinosaurs weighed only half as much as the blue whale. Everything about this animal is on a massive scale. When the blue whale breathes, it releases a jet of water from a blowhole at the top of its head, and its breath is so powerful that the jet can rise up to 40 feet. It would take 34 Asian elephants to match its 170 tons. If the whale were to stand up, it would be as tall as an eight-story building. Its heart weighs as much as an entire cow. Its tongue is nearly as heavy as a van, and its mouth can hold as much water as 450 bathtubs! Only a marine animal could reach these kinds of proportions: On land, its bones could never support the weight, but in the water, it floats.

The most surprising thing about the blue whale is that an animal of such monumental size eats only tiny organisms like krill, a small shrimp not even an inch long. To satisfy its appetite, it has to eat tremendous quantities. It opens its mouth wide and closes it on a group of crustaceans. Then it expels the water from its mouth through its baleen, plates in its mouth that serve as filters, letting the water out, but not the little organisms.

The blue whale is the biggest animal that has ever lived on our planet.

Bigger than the dinosaurs

The hunting of blue whales was banned in 1966 by the International Whaling Commission.

The blue whale is found in all of the planet's oceans.

The blue whale can be found in all of the planet's oceans. Until the late nineteenth and early twentieth centuries, it inhabited them in peace. Things took a turn for the worse with the invention of new, highly effective harpoons for hunting whales of this size. In fifty years, only one in ten blue whales had escaped whalers using these innovative weapons. Since this level of whaling brought the species very close to extinction, it is now totally forbidden to hunt the blue whale. And since the banning of blue whale fishing, the number of blue whales has increased in certain parts of the globe, including off the western coast of North America. This is the least people could do to save this marine mammal, given that our presence on the oceans has exposed it to many additional dangers.

Maritime traffic, which is gradually increasing, is one major problem. Boats pollute the sea by discharging hydrocarbons, but also with the noise they generate, which disturbs whales and dolphins, who are sometimes severely injured in collisions with ships. Even in the ocean, you have to be careful and respect nature . . . especially if you can't see it!

◄ After a year's gestation, a beautiful baby whale extending 16 to 23 feet and weighing 2.75 tons is born. Thanks to its mother's particularly fatty milk, the whale calf will put on 6 to 9 pounds . . . an hour!

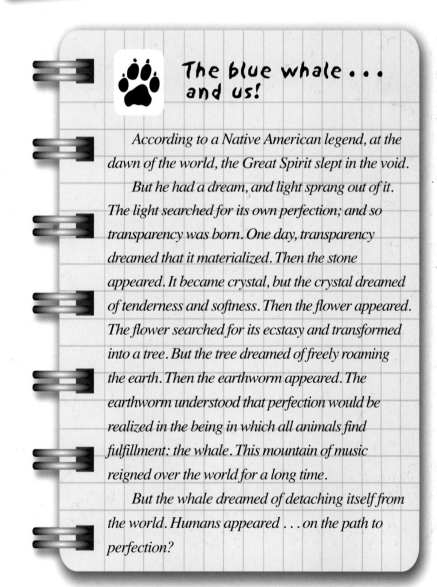

The blue whale . . . and us!

According to a Native American legend, at the dawn of the world, the Great Spirit slept in the void.

But he had a dream, and light sprang out of it. The light searched for its own perfection; and so transparency was born. One day, transparency dreamed that it materialized. Then the stone appeared. It became crystal, but the crystal dreamed of tenderness and softness. Then the flower appeared. The flower searched for its ecstasy and transformed into a tree. But the tree dreamed of freely roaming the earth. Then the earthworm appeared. The earthworm understood that perfection would be realized in the being in which all animals find fulfillment: the whale. This mountain of music reigned over the world for a long time.

But the whale dreamed of detaching itself from the world. Humans appeared . . . on the path to perfection?

The sea otter

The sea otter likes to spend time in the water, but that doesn't prevent it from being sociable. Sometimes it lives in groups of several thousand individuals, when the habitat provides enough food for everyone.

It was long believed that only humans knew how to use tools. But that isn't true. A few animals, such as monkeys, have demonstrated that they know how to take advantage of them. Some birds use twigs to get to caterpillars they cannot reach otherwise. As for the sea otter, it eats shellfish, which it breaks open using stones. It lets itself be carried by the current on its back and smashes its loot against a big rock, held tight against its belly. No shell can resist it!

Unlike other otters, the sea otter lives in the water most of the time and does not need to return to dry land, not even to reproduce. At birth, the sea otter pup does not know how to swim, but the pup's fur traps enough air to keep it at the surface without sinking, like a buoy. When the pup is old enough to dive by itself, at around two months, the layer of air held in its fur diminishes, but it does not disappear entirely since it insulates the diving otter from the freezing water. To reinforce this effect, the tireless little mammal spends hours coating its fur with an oily secretion produced by glands on its skin, which makes it totally waterproof.

The sea otter enjoys a meal while stretched out on its back.

Dangerously precious fur

Some ships carry fuels for us to consume; to limit their trips, we should cut down on car rides and reduce our heating bills.

Sea otters live along the Pacific coastline of North America from Alaska to the Baja Peninsula.

Originally, there were countless sea otters living on the northern coastlines of the Pacific Ocean. Yet the remarkable quality of their fur led them to be hunted close to the point of extinction. A hunting ban has been very successful in bringing about their return, and they have gradually recolonized some of their former territories.

But as soon as one danger disappears, another one appears. When hydrocarbon (oil, gasoline) spills occur after a tanker sinks or cleans out its tanks, they are devastating for sea otters. These substances float at the water's surface and then stick to their fur and alter its insulating effect. Having lost their only protection against the freezing water, they die from the cold. Sometimes, even if they survive the cold, they can be poisoned by absorbing hydrocarbons while grooming themselves.

Hydrocarbon spills are sadly frequent environmental disasters, which have a catastrophic effect on marine fauna and flora. If we want to preserve this fauna and flora, we have to hope that clean and renewable energies will one day replace oil.

◀ The sea otter is so adept at floating on its back and lazing around that it has found a trick to take advantage of the tides without drifting away. When it wants to sleep, it wraps its body in long algae, which anchor it to a fixed point.

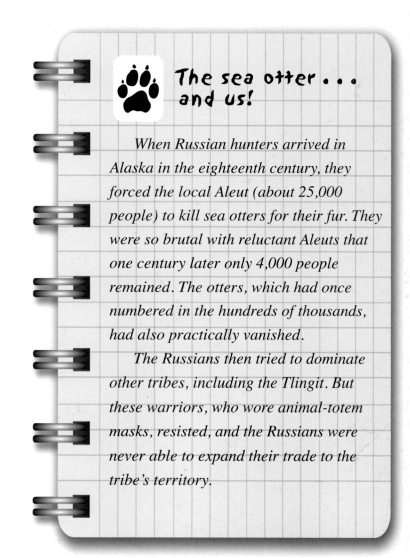

The sea otter... and us!

When Russian hunters arrived in Alaska in the eighteenth century, they forced the local Aleut (about 25,000 people) to kill sea otters for their fur. They were so brutal with reluctant Aleuts that one century later only 4,000 people remained. The otters, which had once numbered in the hundreds of thousands, had also practically vanished.

The Russians then tried to dominate other tribes, including the Tlingit. But these warriors, who wore animal-totem masks, resisted, and the Russians were never able to expand their trade to the tribe's territory.

The black-footed ferret

In order to protect the black-footed ferret, people are working to save its entire ecosystem.

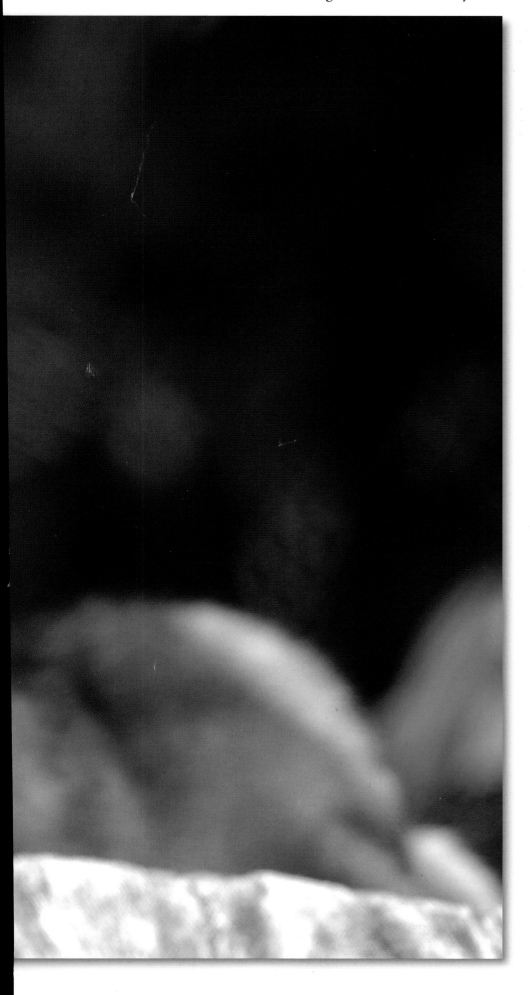

No taller than a stack of eight apples, this little carnivore has champagne-colored fur that darkens to black at its legs and the tip of its tail, and it wears a mask across its face.

The black-footed ferret is part of the same family as otters and weasels. Like them, it has a long body and short legs, handy for moving around inside its den. It lives in the vast prairies of North America but spends most of its time in the tunnels it digs underground, where it sleeps, reproduces, and hunts. It is an intrepid hunter. In fact, its favorite prey, the prairie dog, weighs as much as it does—2 pounds. This masked ferret takes advantage of darkness to go off in search of food.

Guided by its highly acute sense of smell, it locates the prairie dog's distinct odor at the entrance to a burrow and surprises it in its sleep. The ferret's biggest challenge is then to drag its prey back to its own den. Given the size of its catch, it will have enough to eat for at least one week.

The black-footed ferret's favorite prey is the prairie dog, a small North American rodent.

One of the rarest mammals in the world

In general, we throw away too much food and consume too much meat. As a result, intensive agriculture's destructive methods are gaining ground.

The black-footed ferret lives in the plains of North America.

The black-footed ferret is one of the most threatened mammals in North America. It is believed there are only around 1,000 left in the wild. It was even declared extinct in the wild in 1987, a victim of disease and extensive poisoning campaigns aimed at prairie dogs. However, the discovery of a small group of survivors breathed new life into the hope for preservation of the species. A few were raised in captivity, where they reproduced before being reintroduced to their natural habitat. But another threat had appeared: The prairies were being transformed into massive fields as intensive agriculture devastated all natural habitats.

Many species like the black-footed ferret are evicted from their territory by this kind of agricultural expansion. One of the reasons for this expansion is that we consume too much meat, and this consumption leads to intensive breeding of livestock to feed us. The animals in these breeding farms live in poor conditions, and it takes a lot of grain—and thus a lot of fields—to feed them.

Yet there are other types of farming methods—like organic and open air—that are more respectful of animals and the environment. These are better alternatives to factory farming.

◄ The black-footed ferret lives in prairie dogs' burrows—either because the prairie dogs aren't using them or because they became the ferret's prey.

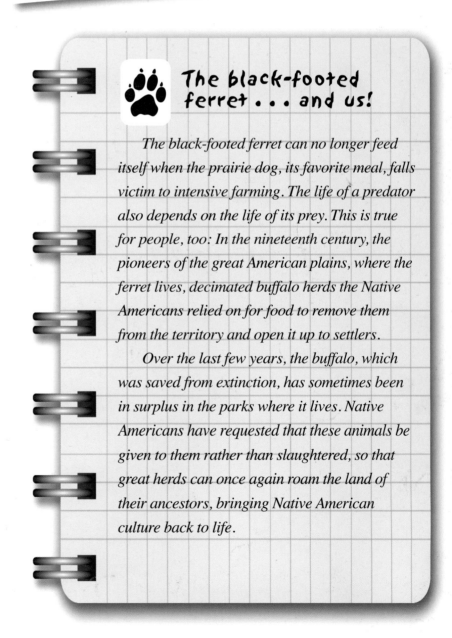

The black-footed ferret . . . and us!

The black-footed ferret can no longer feed itself when the prairie dog, its favorite meal, falls victim to intensive farming. The life of a predator also depends on the life of its prey. This is true for people, too: In the nineteenth century, the pioneers of the great American plains, where the ferret lives, decimated buffalo herds the Native Americans relied on for food to remove them from the territory and open it up to settlers.

Over the last few years, the buffalo, which was saved from extinction, has sometimes been in surplus in the parks where it lives. Native Americans have requested that these animals be given to them rather than slaughtered, so that great herds can once again roam the land of their ancestors, bringing Native American culture back to life.

The monarch

In wintering areas, there are so many monarch butterflies on the trees that sometimes it's difficult to make out a single spot of bark.

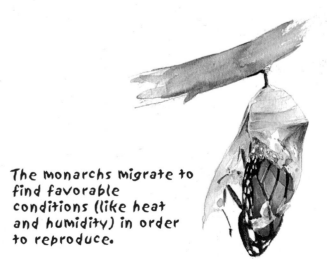

The monarch's migration is probably one of the most beautiful spectacles in nature. Just picture it: Basking in the glow of the sun, a twirling swarm of insects slowly ascends toward the foliage. The pine branches, now sagging under the weight of a legion of butterflies, look like colorful flowers. There are so many butterflies that you can hear them fly: This is known as the "song of the monarchs."

The monarch is a large butterfly, whose delicate black and white patterns stand out elegantly against a bright orange background. Each year, millions of monarchs accomplish an exploit unrivaled in the insect world. They come together to migrate up to 3,100 miles to spend the winter in South America; then their offspring return to spend the summer in North America. What a feat! It is as if all the Americans living east of the Mississippi gathered to migrate to Central America and came home by foot every year.

Once their journey is finished and they have comfortably settled in conifer forests with a hot, humid climate, the monarchs couple. The males die soon after, while the females choose the back of a leaf on which to lay their eggs. These will hatch caterpillars, which turn into chrysalides, and finally butterflies.

The monarchs migrate to find favorable conditions (like heat and humidity) in order to reproduce.

King of the butterflies

The monarchs' wintering area draws thousands of tourists, as well as many scientists, who study them closely. Knowing their behavior can help us save them from disappearing.

NORTH AMERICA

Monarchs spend the summer in North America, then migrate south for the winter.

Monarch migrations are imperiled. Scientists from the International Union for Conservation of Nature have classified them as threatened phenomena.

In the Americas, where these journeys are the most impressive, the monarch's wintering areas have been subjected to massive deforestation.

Yet the tall trees are indispensable for these delicate insects, notably because they protect them from storms. Monarchs are terribly susceptible to cold winds—without shelter they're more likely to die. To make things even more complicated, weeding campaigns are gradually leading to the disappearance of the only plant consumed by the monarch caterpillar: milkweed.

More than one in three invertebrates (animals without spinal columns, such as insects, spiders, worms, and mollusks) is at risk of disappearing. Though they are not very popular, these creatures are highly useful in nature: They pollinate flowers, fertilize soil, transform dead matter into earth, and are at the base of the food chain. Without them, we could not live.

◄ The monarch's beautiful colors warn predators that it is toxic. It acquires this defense by eating milkweed. This plant is vanishing due to intensive agriculture and the pesticides being used, which are endangering the monarch.

The monarch . . . and us!

People are fascinated by butterflies: Hundreds of thousands of tourists travel each year to see the monarchs gather together. Throughout the world, the monarch is considered a magical animal, a symbol of the soul. It represents fairies with their butterfly wings. A Canadian researcher spent thirty-five years trying to figure out where the monarchs he studied spent the winter. It took him twenty years just to invent a tracking device adapted to their wings!

For years, volunteers roamed Mexico until they finally discovered the monarch's wintering zone in 1975. But their mystery is far from being resolved: Why do they migrate? How do they find their way? We still don't have a clue.

The mountain tapir

This tapir lives at high altitudes: Traces of the mountain tapir have been found as high up as 15,400 feet.

The tapir is one of the most curious creatures in nature. This fat, lethargic animal has a funny organ for a nose.

This strange appendage, extending from its upper lip like an elephant's trunk, is highly mobile. The tapir uses it to smell, to turn over soil, and even to move branches aside.

There are four different varieties of tapirs in the world. The mountain tapir is the only one found in the forests and prairies of the Andes Cordillera in South America. These areas are so high up that they are constantly lost in the clouds. The mountain tapir needs a thick coat of woolly fur to fight the cold and humidity.

Another trick to tell it apart from other tapirs: its nearly black fur, which contrasts so much with its white lips that it looks as if it is wearing lipstick!

The tapir's mini-trunk is a real do-it-all tool: Among other things, the tapir uses it to grab plants to eat.

A handy mini-trunk

Nature is a source of dreams and beauty. According to the Wayampi Indians, the tapir gave birth to the Milky Way.

The tapir is found in the forests and prairies of the Andes Cordillera in South America.

The mountain tapir is in danger of extinction. Just think: There are only believed to be less than 2,500 left in the wild. People have always hunted the mountain tapir for its meat and for its leather, for making tools and clothes.

But today the greatest problem facing these shy animals is the destruction of their habitat. The high-altitude forests and prairies of the Andes Cordillera are gradually being turned into fields for growing poppies, building ranches, and raising cattle, or they have become sites of armed conflict.

Conflict has a disastrous impact on the environment. During wars, habitats are razed, laws forbidding illegal trafficking are no longer enforced, and scientists can no longer carry out protection plans.

Throughout the world, countless species have been harmed by conflict, including the okapi in the Democratic Republic of Congo, the elephant at the border of Thailand and Myanmar, and the gorilla in Rwanda.

◀ Despite its clumsy appearance, the tapir is a very bright animal and able to climb up steep slopes by using its long, powerful nails.

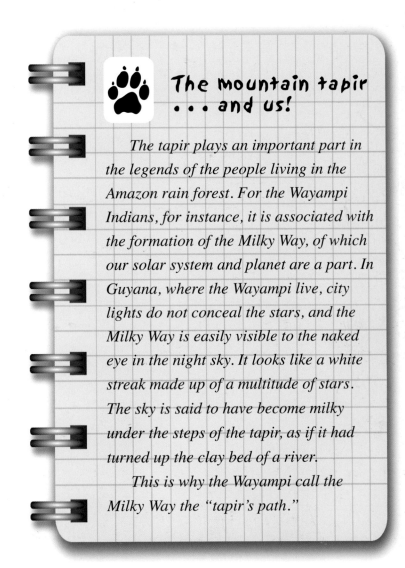

The mountain tapir ... and us!

The tapir plays an important part in the legends of the people living in the Amazon rain forest. For the Wayampi Indians, for instance, it is associated with the formation of the Milky Way, of which our solar system and planet are a part. In Guyana, where the Wayampi live, city lights do not conceal the stars, and the Milky Way is easily visible to the naked eye in the night sky. It looks like a white streak made up of a multitude of stars. The sky is said to have become milky under the steps of the tapir, as if it had turned up the clay bed of a river.

This is why the Wayampi call the Milky Way the "tapir's path."

The spectacled bear

The spectacled bear is essentially a vegetarian. Meat (small rodents, birds, insects) makes up only 5 percent of its diet.

Spectacled bears got their name from the yellow ring patterns around their eyes that make them look as if they are wearing glasses. These patterns vary widely, which is useful for researchers to differentiate the bears when they study them.

You have to look up into the trees to catch a glimpse of this very special bear. Thanks to its powerful claws, this incredible climber can get up above the branches to heights of 30 to 50 feet. It spends much of its time up there looking for food.

Just like the giant panda, this omnivore eats mostly plants. And its favorite foods are often found up in the trees. It likes fruits, berries, and hanging plants like bromeliads. In order to eat its fill, or to wait until the fruit is ripe, it builds a large nest out of dead wood in a fruit tree's branches and settles there for a few days. But it does sometimes come down from its perch. It slowly makes its way to the ground feetfirst, walking backward a little awkwardly. The spectacled bear's quest for food is very useful: It scatters the seeds of the fruits and plants as it eats, and they also wind up in its droppings. This way, it helps the forest to regenerate.

The patterns on spectacled bears' faces vary widely, which makes it easier to differentiate between individuals.

The bear and the tree

The spectacled bear's claws make it easy to climb trees.

The spectacled bear lives on the high mountain slopes of the Andes in South America.

The spectacled bear lives on the high mountain slopes of the Andes in South America, where it is found in different types of habitats, such as prairies and forests with varying degrees of humidity. But these areas are increasingly inhabited by people, who are daily cutting down on the size of the bears' territory by clearing and cultivating it or having cattle graze there.

The spectacled bear is also hunted for its meat, fur, claws, fat, and bile (secreted by the liver, it helps the bear to digest food), which is sometimes used in traditional medicine in certain countries.

The use of animal derivatives in pharmaceuticals is common all over the world and unfortunately encourages the illegal trade of endangered species. Asian folk remedies, for example, call for the rhinoceros horn to fight fever, tiger bones to combat a whole string of illnesses, and powdered seahorses for circulation problems. The worst thing is that often these products have no effect at all.

◀ The young are born during the season when the fruit ripens. Thanks to this food, their mother will be able to keep them well nourished.

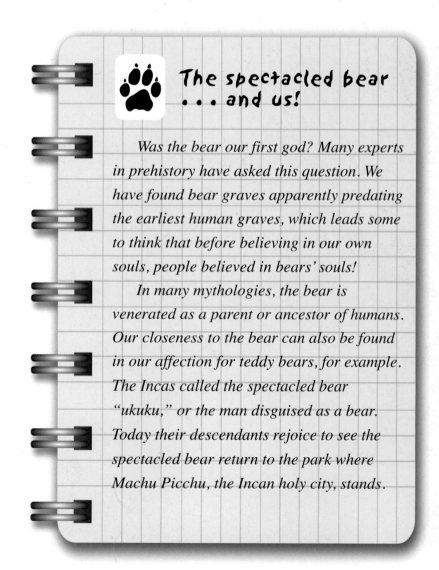

The spectacled bear ... and us!

Was the bear our first god? Many experts in prehistory have asked this question. We have found bear graves apparently predating the earliest human graves, which leads some to think that before believing in our own souls, people believed in bears' souls!

In many mythologies, the bear is venerated as a parent or ancestor of humans. Our closeness to the bear can also be found in our affection for teddy bears, for example. The Incas called the spectacled bear "ukuku," or the man disguised as a bear. Today their descendants rejoice to see the spectacled bear return to the park where Machu Picchu, the Incan holy city, stands.

91

The hyacinth macaw

With their long tails floating behind them like banners, hyacinth macaws fly in pairs, keeping in contact via their calls as they cover great distances.

The biggest parrot in the world is blue—completely blue—with the exception of the bright yellow skin around its eyes and beak. Its size, its wingspan (which stretches nearly as wide as the outspread arms of a grown man), its unusually colored plumage, and its very long tail certainly make it one of the most beautiful of all parrots.

A great appreciator of palm fruit, it gorges itself on all kinds of nuts. It has an unbeatable tool to break these fruits' extremely tough shells: its beak.

Though the hyacinth macaw is impressively big, its ability to apply pressure is surprising for an animal that only weighs 3¼ pounds. Since parrots spend most of their time nibbling, the edges of their beaks are as sharp as knife blades and never stop growing, which prevents potential wear and tear. But breaking nuts isn't the beak's only purpose. The hyacinth macaw's beak also serves as an extra limb and can be used to climb, smooth out its feathers, feed its young, and attack or caress its fellow birds. Since it is sensitive to touch, the parrot also uses it to explore its surroundings.

The trees in which hyacinth macaws build their nests are being cut down to make pastures. Artificial nests are built so that hyacinth macaws can keep reproducing.

The "blue parrot"

Beware of trends: The animals we choose for domestic pets are not always suited for that kind of life. Removing macaws from their natural habitat can affect their environment and fellow creatures.

The hyacinth macaw lives in South America, in Brazil, Paraguay, and Bolivia.

The beauty of these splendid birds has cost them their numbers. They were still abundant a few decades ago, but their population has dropped radically, to the point that today there are only about 6,500 in the wild. A growing number of poachers continue to capture these birds to sell them as pets. Their decline has happened so quickly that international authorities have taken measures to ban their capture completely and regulate trade. But these steps still aren't sufficient; the hyacinth macaw continues to be hunted down for illegal trade, and their numbers in the wild will continue to drop unless something more can be done.

Millions of birds are captured each year to be sold as pets and put in cages. The harsh reality is that many animals die after they are captured or while being transported. As a result, a number of governments signed an agreement regulating international trade in threatened species called the CITES convention (the Convention on International Trade in Endangered Species of Wild Fauna and Flora) in 1973.

◄ The hyacinth macaw's beak is so strong that it can even crack open coconuts.

The hyacinth macaw ...and us!

In the wild, hyacinth macaws live in groups, notably because of their need to communicate with each other. They can talk, sing, dance, chew (though they have no teeth), play . . .

They are also very sensitive and get particularly unhappy about "falling out" with their fellow creatures. They don't like being far from them.

This is yet another reason to avoid taking them from their habitats and their families. Birds are made to fly and be free: They are not toys or decorative objects. Some parrots are even more intelligent than three-year-old children!

The golden lion tamarin

As its name suggests, the golden lion tamarin is quite ferocious. When in danger, it bristles its mane, bares its teeth, makes strident cries, and gets ready to bite.

The most striking quality of the golden lion tamarin is its opulent mane, reminiscent of a lion's. It doesn't exactly keep a low profile with that brilliant orange fur—except perhaps in the trees, where it blends in with ripe fruit and dead leaves in the sunlight.

Like other primates—including humans—these small monkeys have hands with a thumb and four digits. Since they love to eat insects, their hands have evolved so that they're able to catch them in crevices or in the ground. Their palms and index fingers are very thin and extended, which allow them to fit into narrow openings, where tasty little bugs generally hide. However, their diet isn't exclusively composed of insects: Golden lion tamarins also love fruit.

In order to stay hydrated, they drink the water held in the leaves of plants growing in trees. If they can't find any, they bite into certain vines, whose sap is very thirst-quenching.

To avoid climbing down to the ground, golden lion tamarins drink water held in leaves.

A little monkey that makes a big impression

The golden lion tamarin lives in the Atlantic Forest, a rain forest in Brazil that stretches along the Atlantic Ocean. It is one of the most threatened forests in the world, but also one of the richest in animal and plant species. People have exploited it so much (for charcoal or to turn it into fields and pastures) that when you look at satellite images, you can only see little parcels of it scattered across the map. Imagine a pizza representing the Atlantic Forest's original surface. Cut it into ten equal slices. The only thing left today is a single slice!

A few years ago, there were hardly any golden lion tamarins left in the wild, so scientists began to reintroduce them. This initiative was successful at first, but the forest is so fragmented that the population can hardly grow. A solution used in similar cases could improve this species' situation: the creation of "biological corridors," or nature reserves connected to each other by strips of protected land, which allow animals to circulate and meet.

◀ The female golden lion tamarin gives birth to twins or triplets. They will then largely be raised and carried with the help of their father and with the assistance of other members of the family.

The golden lion tamarin lives in the Atlantic Forest in Brazil.

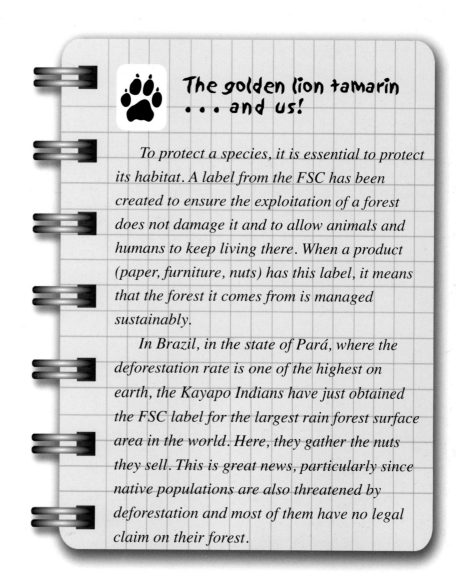

The golden lion tamarin ... and us!

To protect a species, it is essential to protect its habitat. A label from the FSC has been created to ensure the exploitation of a forest does not damage it and to allow animals and humans to keep living there. When a product (paper, furniture, nuts) has this label, it means that the forest it comes from is managed sustainably.

In Brazil, in the state of Pará, where the deforestation rate is one of the highest on earth, the Kayapo Indians have just obtained the FSC label for the largest rain forest surface area in the world. Here, they gather the nuts they sell. This is great news, particularly since native populations are also threatened by deforestation and most of them have no legal claim on their forest.

The Amazon river dolphin

The Amazon river dolphin's nose is covered in vibrissa (much like cats' whiskers) that help it to find its way in muddy water. But like all dolphins, it also relies on echolocation (it sends out sounds and listens to their echo).

During the rainy season, rivers and streams in South America swell and flood much of the forest. During this time, Amazon river dolphins love to venture into the woods. In order to slip between tree trunks and roots, their necks have become highly flexible, so they can turn their heads in every direction. And since it isn't easy to swim in shallow water, their dorsal fin has been reduced to a simple bump. This way they don't get it caught in the branches when swimming backward. They eat crabs, turtles, and especially fish, including the infamous piranha.

In order to capture prey hidden in the tangle of roots, the river dolphin's jaws transformed into a kind of long beak with anywhere from 50 to 70 little teeth. Not bad compared to a human, who only has 32!

Amazon river dolphins are highly intelligent creatures, with a brain capacity 40 percent larger than that of humans.

The mysterious freshwater dolphin

When the extraction of gold contaminates the environment, the precious metal becomes a poisoned chalice.

The Amazon river dolphin lives in the rivers of South America, throughout the Orinoco and Amazon river basins.

There are several species of freshwater dolphin, found in China, India, and South America. Though we know very little about the Amazon river dolphin, scientists know of its threatened status.

Often a victim of human activities (hit by boats, isolated by hydroelectric dams, caught in fishing nets, hunted by fishermen, etc.), it is especially vulnerable to the pollution of the Amazon River—as are many other species.

Despite a strict ban on the practice, many gold miners use mercury to extract the precious metal. Even in small doses, mercury is highly toxic. It always gets discharged into the rivers in the extraction process. The entire food chain is contaminated, right up to mankind! The Indians who bathe in the river, drink its water, and eat its fish are now sick because of the mercury.

◀ Freshwater dolphins are clever animals that can leap up to 3 feet out of the water and swim on their backs . . . just like any other dolphin!

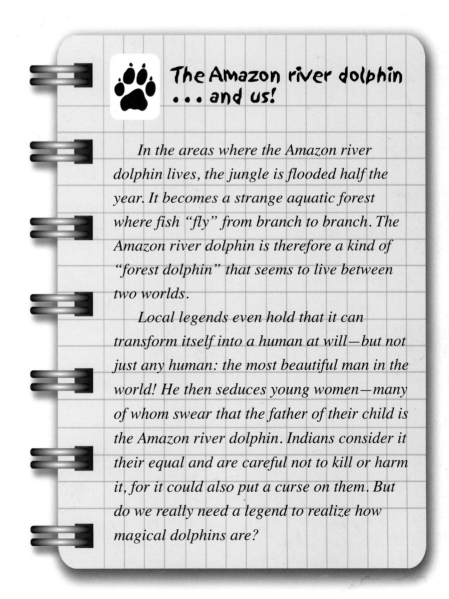

The Amazon river dolphin . . . and us!

In the areas where the Amazon river dolphin lives, the jungle is flooded half the year. It becomes a strange aquatic forest where fish "fly" from branch to branch. The Amazon river dolphin is therefore a kind of "forest dolphin" that seems to live between two worlds.

Local legends even hold that it can transform itself into a human at will—but not just any human: the most beautiful man in the world! He then seduces young women—many of whom swear that the father of their child is the Amazon river dolphin. Indians consider it their equal and are careful not to kill or harm it, for it could also put a curse on them. But do we really need a legend to realize how magical dolphins are?

The maned wolf

Maned wolf cubs have very dark fur, but the tip of their tail is white. As they grow, they turn a magnificent tawny color, but their nose, mane, and feet remain black.

Contrary to what its name suggests, the maned wolf is not a wolf. Nor is it a fox, a coyote, a dog, or a jackal. Instead, it is a member of the Canidae family, which is divided into "wolf-like" and "dog-like" animals. Equipped with long legs, this animal roams the grassy plains of South America. But this was not always the case.

Originally great carnivores, maned wolves have become mostly omnivores. Although they sometimes eat small prey (typically rodents, hares, birds, and fish), the majority of their diet consists of roots, berries, vegetables, and fruits. Their morphology has also changed: Their legs have extended so they can see over tall grasses. Their fur has turned red so they can go unnoticed among the amber colors of the dried leaves. They've lost the insulation beneath their fur so they can withstand the torrid heat. And their ears have grown large so they can easily hear their prey without needing to see them.

Its black mane allows the maned wolf to look more imposing when it bristles.

An unusual species

Stories of werewolves and the "big bad wolf" can give real wolves—and their cousin, the maned wolf—a bad reputation.

SOUTH AMERICA

The maned wolf lives in the south of Brazil and Paraguay, the north of Argentina, Bolivia, and Peru.

The principal threat to the maned wolf is the expansion of agriculture. Intensive agriculture is on the rise in areas where this unusual species lives. This type of farming is characterized by massive fields, which are abundantly treated with fertilizer and pesticides (to destroy parasitic animals) so the plants will grow more quickly. But these practices are dangerous for the surrounding flora and fauna. Intensive agriculture continually pushes back the edges of wild species' territories, while the toxic products it uses poison living creatures.

This is why there's growing enthusiasm for organic farming. It replaces synthetic chemical products with natural methods. To fertilize the soil, farmers use manure or let the land lie fallow temporarily (meaning the ground is given time to rest). Similarly, to fight against insect invasions, organic farmers avoid using any pesticides, instead encouraging the presence of birds, small mammals, and predatory insects, notably by maintaining hedges where they can live.

◄The search for food leads the maned wolf to travel an average of 18 miles a day.

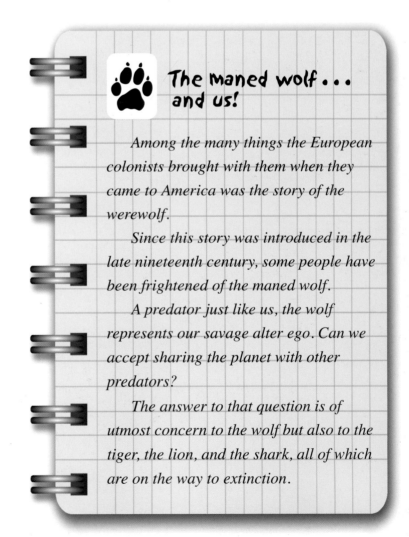

The maned wolf... and us!

Among the many things the European colonists brought with them when they came to America was the story of the werewolf.

Since this story was introduced in the late nineteenth century, some people have been frightened of the maned wolf.

A predator just like us, the wolf represents our savage alter ego. Can we accept sharing the planet with other predators?

The answer to that question is of utmost concern to the wolf but also to the tiger, the lion, and the shark, all of which are on the way to extinction.

The black-and-white ruffed lemur

How are the ruffed lemur and the tiger alike? Their fur! The contrast between dark and light in their coats allows them both to hide in the shadowy patterns of their respective forests.

Like monkeys and humans, the lemur is a primate. Like humans, it has hands with opposable thumbs. This is how it takes hold of objects with such skill. Most lemurs are found on Madagascar, an island off the southeastern coast of Africa. One theory holds that several million years ago, small lemurs crossed the channel separating the African continent from the island by sailing on natural rafts such as tree trunks and plants. Once they came to dry land, they adapted to the totally isolated island so well that, with time, they evolved into more than seventy different species.

The quiet black-and-white ruffed lemur is perfectly adapted to the rain forests it calls home. Because of its very dense fur, its coat protects it from the frequent downpours that regularly soak the forest.

After a rainy night, it finds a sunny spot and sits with its arms spread out to warm its belly. And when the lemur balances on thin tree branches, its long tail serves as a pole to steady itself and prevent falls.

To warm up, ruffed lemurs expose the black fur of their bellies as soon as the sun rises.

An adorable lemur

Ecotourism in places like Madagascar can stimulate local economies while still respecting animals' habitats.

The lemur lives on Madagascar, an island off the southeastern coast of Africa.

The forest in Madagascar is one of the richest environments for species. But its trees are being cut down and burned in such high numbers that the forest's surface area is quickly dwindling. When tree roots disappear, nothing holds the soil in place, and it is carried away by streams, then rivers, and finally the sea.

When people first arrived in Madagascar, there were many more lemur species than there are today. But deforestation and intensive lemur hunting have led to the extinction of at least fifteen of these species.

People have hunted many animals to the point of extinction. Just two of the many animals that disappeared less than 100 years ago are the Barbary lion, a magnificent wild beast that lived in the mountains of North Africa, and the Tasmanian wolf, a carnivore that had a pouch on its belly to carry its young, just like the kangaroo.

◀ Lemurs' hands and feet have five thin digits, one of which is opposable to the others and all of which have nails. Their second finger even has a claw, which makes scratching that much easier.

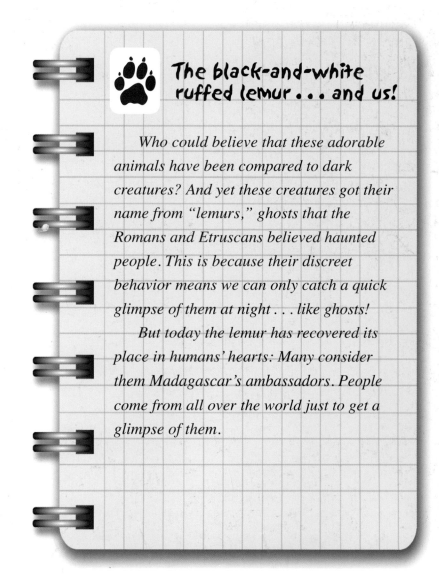

The black-and-white ruffed lemur . . . and us!

Who could believe that these adorable animals have been compared to dark creatures? And yet these creatures got their name from "lemurs," ghosts that the Romans and Etruscans believed haunted people. This is because their discreet behavior means we can only catch a quick glimpse of them at night . . . like ghosts!

But today the lemur has recovered its place in humans' hearts: Many consider them Madagascar's ambassadors. People come from all over the world just to get a glimpse of them.

The Western lowland gorilla

The Western lowland gorilla's gender and age determine its coat's appearance. Older males develop a silvery gray fur on their back. There is only one "silver back" in each group: the dominant male.

Gorillas are among the "great apes" (like the chimpanzee and the orangutan). Like all great apes, they are not only big, they also share many traits in common with humans. No surprise there, since we have a single ancestor: the primate. The great apes' shared characteristics with humans are a highly developed brain, the ability to walk on their two hind limbs, and a thumb to skillfully take hold of objects.

Looking at Western lowland gorillas, one is immediately struck by how much they resemble humans. Their hairless faces make it easy to see their expressions and even identify their emotions. But the most amazing fact is how intelligent these gorillas are. In the wild, they communicate by using a language consisting of more than one hundred gestures, which are understood by all other gorillas, even those that have never been in contact with them.

The gorilla is exclusively vegetarian. It eats a lot of plants for nourishment.

So similar to us!

The famous primatologist Dian Fossey interacts with a band of gorillas.

Western lowland gorillas live in the rain forests and swamps of West Africa.

In the last thirty years, the population of Western lowland gorillas has dropped by more than half. What's the reason for the rapid decline?

The Western lowland gorilla inhabits the humid and swampy rain forests of West Africa. Since the 1980s, exploitation by the timber industry has increased tremendously. Sadly, this activity not only is responsible for the decrease in forests, it also creates routes for people and disease to gain access to an otherwise impenetrable environment. Humans have taken advantage of this to hunt the great ape and sell its meat. And the Ebola virus has proved to be as deadly to apes as it is to people.

In Africa, often impoverished local populations are in the habit of eating "the meat of the bush" — in other words, the wild animals they find in the forest. Unfortunately, a constantly growing population requires a growing number of animals to satisfy the demand. It has been suggested that a possible solution to this problem would be to have local populations manage forests themselves so that they can sustainably provide people with what they need to live.

◄ To get rid of intestinal parasites, gorillas swallow thorny leaves rich in tannin without chewing them. Very effective medicine!

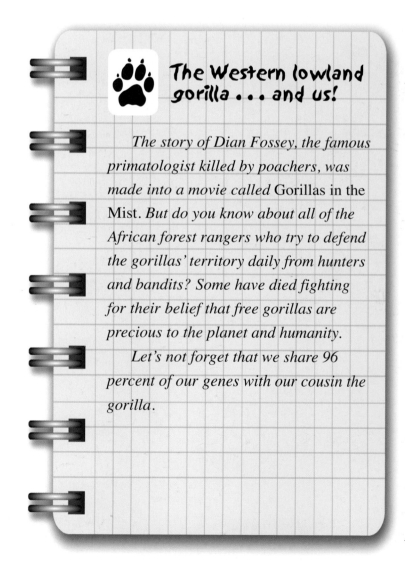

The Western lowland gorilla ... and us!

The story of Dian Fossey, the famous primatologist killed by poachers, was made into a movie called Gorillas in the Mist. *But do you know about all of the African forest rangers who try to defend the gorillas' territory daily from hunters and bandits? Some have died fighting for their belief that free gorillas are precious to the planet and humanity.*

Let's not forget that we share 96 percent of our genes with our cousin the gorilla.

The Ethiopian wolf

Ethiopian wolf cubs are cared for and fed by the entire pack. Once they are six months old, they start accompanying the adults on their rounds to monitor their territory.

The Ethiopian wolf's flaming red and white fur, powerful long legs, and thin nose give it a natural elegance.

Living at altitudes of more than 9,800 feet, this carnivore roams the Ethiopian highlands' cold prairies. Like all other wolves, it lives in packs. Every morning and every night, the adults come together to make the rounds of their territory.

Hunting, however, is a solitary activity. In these short grass prairies the wolves' favorite prey is the giant mole rat, which is easier to flush out alone rather than as a pack. The Ethiopian wolf has two tactics: either dig up the rodent's burrow with its paws or simply lie in wait.

After having spotted the mole rat at the entrance of its hideout, the Ethiopian wolf lies low in the grass, then, while staying close to the ground, creeps forward the moment its victim turns its back. Once it is near the hole, it leaps on the rat. No need for ten wolves to do this job.

The Ethiopian wolf has two methods to hunt its favorite prey, the giant mole rat: lying in wait or digging up its burrow.

117

A beautiful wolf with flaming red fur

Like all wolves, Ethiopian wolves live together in packs.

The Ethiopian wolf roams the Ethiopian highlands at altitudes above 9,800 feet.

The Ethiopian wolf is the rarest wolf of all: There are only 500 left. Though we often don't think about it, pets can be a real danger to wild fauna. This is the case for the Ethiopian wolf, which recently lost a quarter of its population to a rabies epidemic. Major rabies vaccination campaigns have been organized to try to save these animals.

Dogs raised by humans can carry diseases, but that's not all they pass on. Dogs and wolves are very similar animals and can reproduce together. The young born of the union between a wolf and a dog are half-wolf, half-dog and are no longer like the wild species.

A great number of other animals are imperiled by the presence of species introduced into environments where they do not belong. They throw ecosystems off balance so radically that this problem has become the second leading cause of extinction after habitat modification.

◄ At an average of 23 inches to the shoulder and 35 pounds, the Ethiopian wolf isn't very big. But you can't miss their power when a few of them get together: They live in small packs of three to thirteen adults and don't like competition.

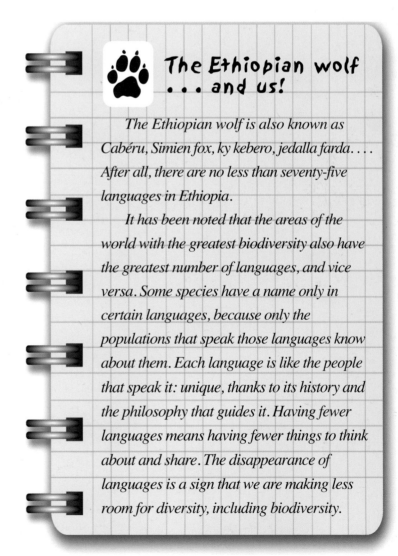

The Ethiopian wolf . . . and us!

The Ethiopian wolf is also known as Cabéru, Simien fox, ky kebero, jedalla farda. . . . After all, there are no less than seventy-five languages in Ethiopia.

It has been noted that the areas of the world with the greatest biodiversity also have the greatest number of languages, and vice versa. Some species have a name only in certain languages, because only the populations that speak those languages know about them. Each language is like the people that speak it: unique, thanks to its history and the philosophy that guides it. Having fewer languages means having fewer things to think about and share. The disappearance of languages is a sign that we are making less room for diversity, including biodiversity.

The sawfish

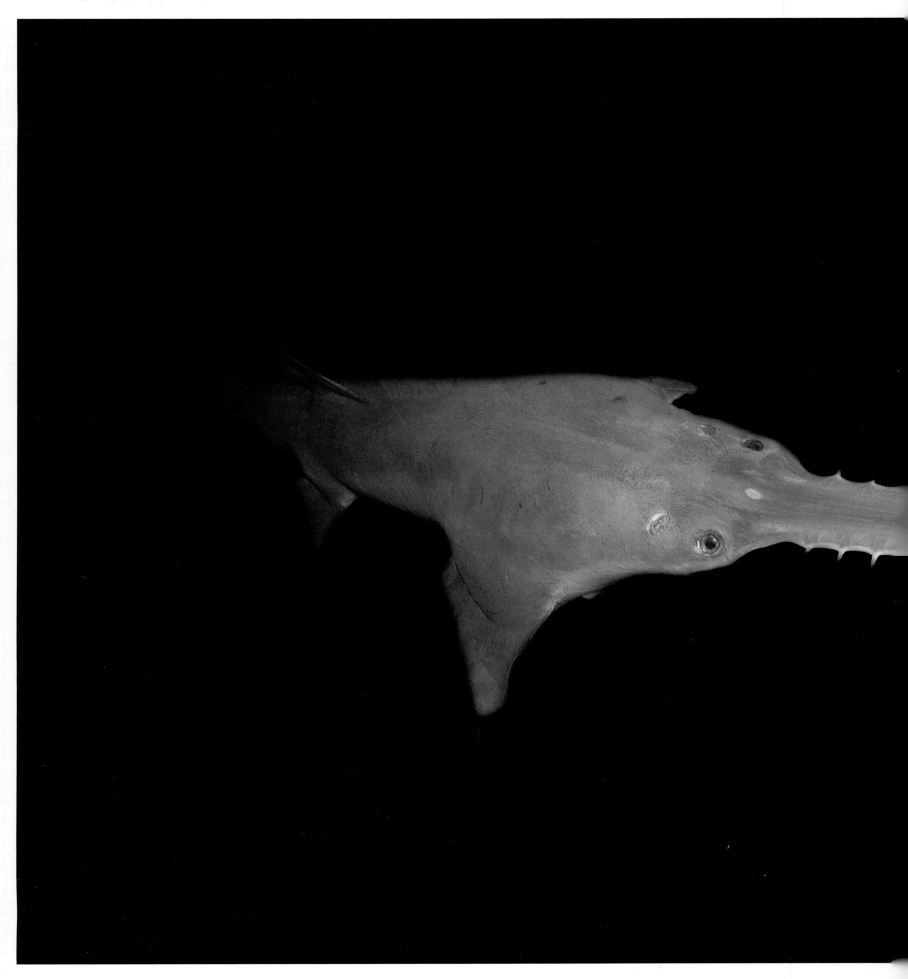

The sawfish can live both in salt and freshwater, so long as the water is shallow and it can find a sandy or muddy bottom.

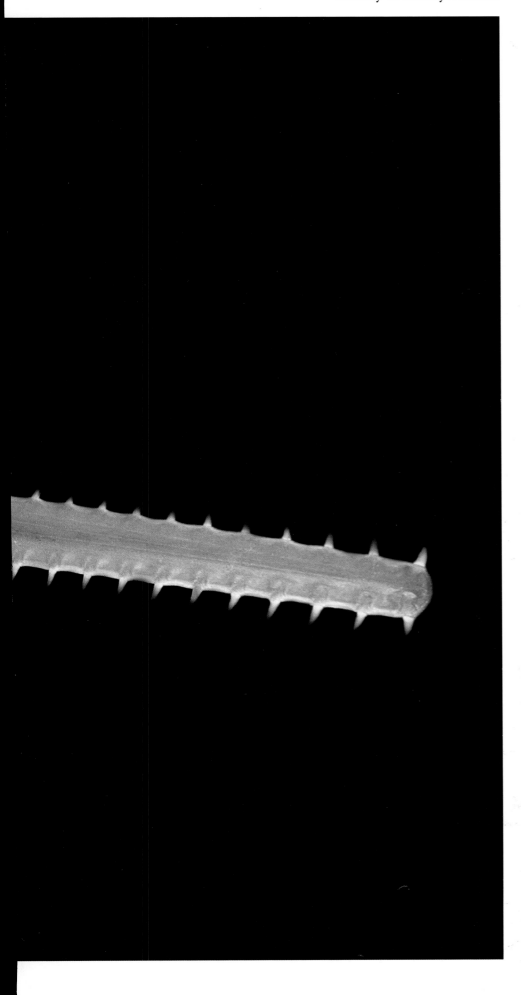

A fish with a saw instead of a nose . . . what a strange trick of nature! Of course, it isn't really a saw and its function is not at all like the tool after which it is named. In fact, it is a bony extension of the animal's rostrum, or its nose. Its dimensions can be truly impressive, stretching up to 6½ feet (bigger than the height of an average man). Depending on the species, the sawfish can have from 18 to 37 teeth along each side of its rostrum . . . along with a few in its mouth! This strange instrument helps it to catch its prey. It uses it to comb the sandy river bottom to unearth crustaceans and shrimp or to impale fish. Pretty clever, right?

This strange fish grows slowly, but very old members of some species can measure up to 25 feet, or the equivalent of a three-story building! It is similar to sharks and skates. In fact, its body looks like a flatter version of a shark's. Not surprisingly for an animal that spends its time at the bottom of the water, but no deeper than 330 feet, the sawfish prefers to stay in bays, estuaries, and even rivers.

The sawfish is related to the shark and the skate.

A fish to set your teeth on edge

The MSC label (Marine Stewardship Council) means that the fish you are buying comes from fisheries that do not destroy ecosystems and that preserve species.

The sawfish lives in tropical and subtropical waters, salt and freshwater.

The sawfish is among the most threatened fish in the world. It has already vanished from many of its former marine territories. Like most species, it is imperiled by the degradation of its habitat. Since it lives very close to coastlines, it is heavily affected by human activity and pollution. But the biggest danger for this fish is fishing, whether intentional or accidental. When a sawfish finds itself caught in a fishing net, its rostrum gets twisted up in the meshes, and it is impossible for it to free itself.

Traditional fishing is very common in Africa. This ancestral activity has significantly developed in recent years with growing demand and increasingly poor populations of fishermen. Furthermore, commercial factory ships from the richest countries also come to catch massive numbers of fish, which are therefore becoming increasingly rare. These ships fish without making any distinction between their prey, occasionally even scraping the ocean floor. They then throw out a good portion of their catch . . . now dead. Thankfully, some fisheries have decided to promote the MSC label, which guarantees that the fishing was respectful of all species and the environment.

◀ The slits on the underside of the sawfish are its gills. The location of the gills indicates that the fish is part of the skate family. If these gills were on its side, it would be part of the shark family.

The sawfish . . . and us!

In African mythologies, the sawfish is a symbol of fertility and prosperity. Fishermen understand why the sawfish is disappearing: Pushed to compete with each other, some fishermen are using increasingly aggressive methods to find fish. To help the fish recover their numbers, many have agreed not to catch overly young fish and to leave species alone during their mating seasons, so they can develop in peace. The riches of the sawfish are much greater than a mere bank bill.

The dwarf crocodile

Unlike other crocodiles, the dwarf crocodile prefers to spend its days in the shade, hidden along the banks of rivers and in holes it digs for itself.

The dwarf crocodile lives in the swamps of the African rain forest. No longer than 6½ feet, it may not be a large crocodile, but beware: It is an aggressive one!

Still, the female dwarf crocodile is a very caring mother. When she's ready to lay her eggs, she carefully chooses the ideal place to make her nest. It has to be humid, but not too much, so the eggs don't rot, and hot enough so that the eggs incubate at an average temperature of 86°F.

Once she's chosen a spot, she gets to work building a large mound out of plants. She'll then lay about ten eggs at the bottom of the mound. After they've been covered up, they will incubate for three months in the moisture of the decomposing plants and under the mother's careful attention. When they hatch, the young immediately begin to vocalize. The female responds by helping to haul them out of the nest. They are only about 11 inches long at this point.

The mother will keep watching over them for a long time, fending predators off, carrying them in her mouth, or guiding them toward swimming areas, until they venture out into a new life.

Young dwarf crocodiles vocalize to notify their mother when they are ready to come out of their egg.

A caring mother

Some of the clothing we wear—like leather and fur—is harmful to animals. It's also harmful when intensive farming is used to produce cotton. When given the option, it is better to wear linen, hemp, wool, or organic cotton.

The dwarf crocodile can be found in the rainforests of West Central Africa.

Hidden in the marshlands of the lush African rain forest, dwarf crocodiles are hard to study. We don't really know how many are currently alive. However, judging by how fast their forest is being destroyed and the phenomenal quantity of these reptiles sold on markets, it seems obvious that the species is imperiled.

According to the International Union for Conservation of Nature's Red List of Threatened Species, 28 percent of the reptiles on the planet are threatened, or more than one in four! Powerless before the destruction of their habitat (deforestation, soil and water pollution, road construction), they also have to face illegal trade, whether for their skin, their meat, alleged medical purposes, or to be turned into pets. Unfortunately, these species reproduce very late (at ten, fifteen, or twenty years old among certain turtles and certain crocodiles). Their reproduction is therefore increasingly compromised, and their numbers are dwindling far too quickly.

◄ The dwarf crocodile is a solitary and nocturnal animal. During the day it digs out a burrow in which to hide and sleep.

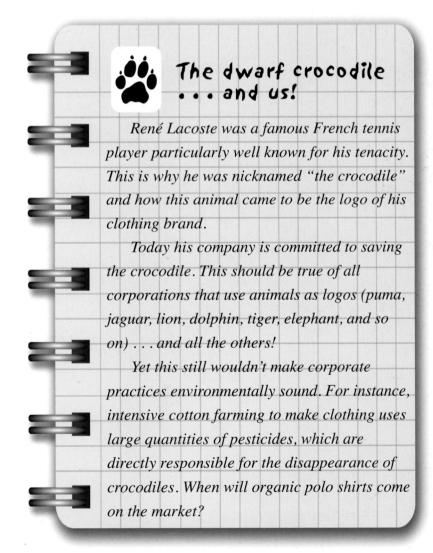

The dwarf crocodile . . . and us!

René Lacoste was a famous French tennis player particularly well known for his tenacity. This is why he was nicknamed "the crocodile" and how this animal came to be the logo of his clothing brand.

Today his company is committed to saving the crocodile. This should be true of all corporations that use animals as logos (puma, jaguar, lion, dolphin, tiger, elephant, and so on) . . . and all the others!

Yet this still wouldn't make corporate practices environmentally sound. For instance, intensive cotton farming to make clothing uses large quantities of pesticides, which are directly responsible for the disappearance of crocodiles. When will organic polo shirts come on the market?

The West African giraffe

The giraffe is about 6 feet tall and weighs from 100 to 150 pounds at birth. It is able to run only a few hours after it comes out of its mother's belly!

Standing 18 feet tall, the giraffe is like the earth's giant: as tall as two Asian elephants standing on top of each other!

Its neck is impressively long. How many vertebrae does it have? The answer is seven, the same number we have in our necks. But the giraffe is cheating, because each of its vertebrae is up to 15 inches long. The giraffe also has a long blue tongue that helps it reach the tops of trees, where the most tender leaves are found. It is so tall that it needs an enormous heart—thirty times the size of a human one—to send blood all the way to its brain! Everything about the giraffe is oversize. The most incredible fact is that when a baby giraffe is born, it is already the size and weight of an adult man! And when it comes out of its mother, it drops 6½ feet. Quite the fall.

The West African giraffe lives in Niger, in the African Sahel, where the rainy season is so short that the few trees that grow there are nearly constantly covered in a thick cream-colored dust. This is probably why the giants you find here have such light coats compared to other giraffes: They have adapted to better camouflage themselves.

The giraffe's long blue tongue is tough enough that it can handle the sharp thorns on trees.

Such a big heart!

Like the wolf and the tiger, the white giraffe is something of a symbol for the struggle to find a life in which people are in harmony with nature.

The white giraffe lives in Niger, in the African Sahel of West Africa.

The few West African giraffes living to the south of the capital of Niger are the last tower of giraffes in West Africa. (A group of giraffes is known as a "tower of giraffes.") They are also the last of this subspecies to live in total freedom, roaming through the pastures and fields. In this area where local populations are extremely poor, cohabitation with people is often very difficult. Villagers cut down trees to feed their herds or to use as firewood. Due to lack of food, giraffes are driven by hunger to eat crops.

About a decade ago, human pressure led the giraffe population in Niger to drop to fifty individuals. But thanks to the dedicated work of a Nigerien organization, the number of these herbivores has more than tripled since then.

The organization's activities are simple: It helps villagers by developing ecotourism or giving them microloans to invest in wells or grain mills. In exchange, villagers commit to protecting the giraffes.

◀ Giraffes love to eat acacia leaves, but sometimes they snack on the local cowpea crop (a kind of bean).

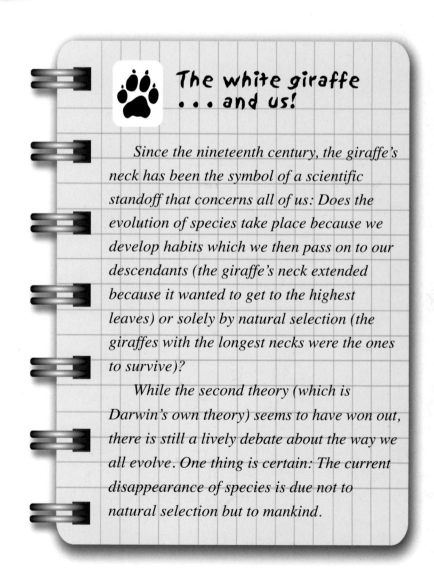

The white giraffe ... and us!

Since the nineteenth century, the giraffe's neck has been the symbol of a scientific standoff that concerns all of us: Does the evolution of species take place because we develop habits which we then pass on to our descendants (the giraffe's neck extended because it wanted to get to the highest leaves) or solely by natural selection (the giraffes with the longest necks were the ones to survive)?

While the second theory (which is Darwin's own theory) seems to have won out, there is still a lively debate about the way we all evolve. One thing is certain: The current disappearance of species is due not to natural selection but to mankind.

The great hammerhead

The great hammerhead is a rather solitary animal.

What use could that unusual hammer-shaped head possibly have? Scientists have wondered about it for decades. Turns out, the position of the hammerhead shark's eyes on the sides of its head gives it exceptional vision. Its depth perception is better than other marine animals, but it also gains a panoramic visual field by moving its head and eyes. In other words, it can see all around it without having to twist its body.

Hunting at dusk, the hammerhead shark also uses a sixth sense to spot its prey: Cells beneath its head can detect the minute electrical fields naturally produced by any living being. This characteristic allows it to locate prey such as small fish, other sharks, and sometimes even crustaceans and squid. But its favorite food is undoubtedly the skate. It loves it so much that it has become immune to its venom. If a person were to be stung by a skate, he or she would experience terrible pain and feel nauseous for more than two hours!

The great hammerhead shark's favorite prey is the skate, which is also threatened by overfishing.

A hammer to see better!

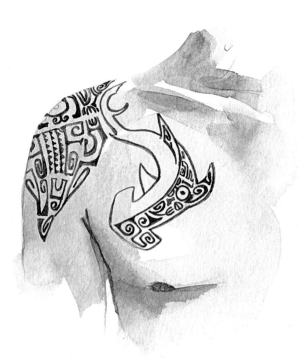

The hammerhead shark is a very common design in Polynesian tattoos: It symbolizes justice, wisdom, and protection.

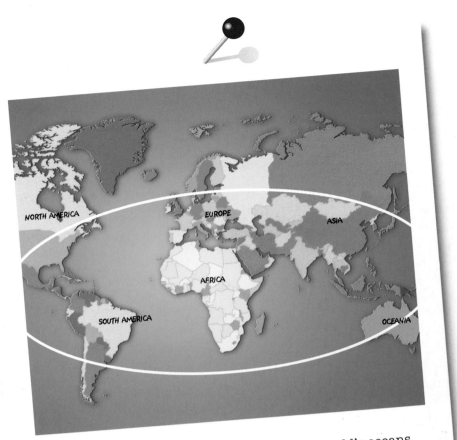

The hammerhead shark roams all of the world's oceans.

Overfishing is the principal cause of the decline of the great hammerhead shark. It is hunted by fishermen who value its meat, as its large fins are particularly sought after by lovers of Asian cuisine. Great hammerhead sharks are also regularly caught accidentally in fishermen's nets, getting their long fins and big head tangled up. This species takes a while to reach maturity and reproduces in small numbers. Humans are harvesting far too many of them given the low frequency of births, to the point that it is now believed that the total population has declined significantly, particularly along the coast of western Africa, where the population has dropped by nearly 80 percent in barely twenty-five years!

Some measures have been passed to save the hammerhead shark, but the greatest difficulty at the moment is enforcing the law.

Unfortunately, all the great marine predators are facing the same fate despite the major role they play in the marine environment: They maintain the balance between different species.

◀ Underwater, the hammerhead shark is easily recognizable by its head. But it can also be identified when its highly developed fin pokes through the surface of the water.

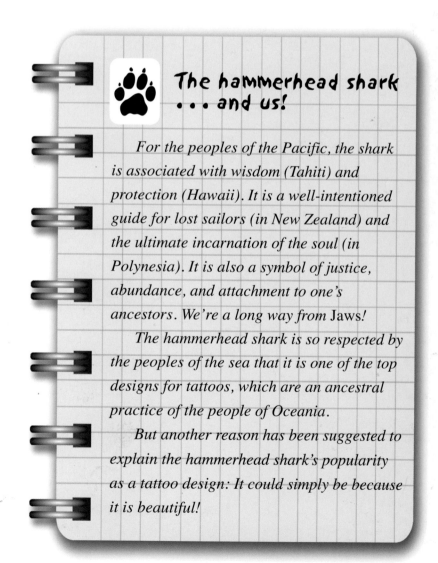

The hammerhead shark ... and us!

For the peoples of the Pacific, the shark is associated with wisdom (Tahiti) and protection (Hawaii). It is a well-intentioned guide for lost sailors (in New Zealand) and the ultimate incarnation of the soul (in Polynesia). It is also a symbol of justice, abundance, and attachment to one's ancestors. We're a long way from Jaws!

The hammerhead shark is so respected by the peoples of the sea that it is one of the top designs for tattoos, which are an ancestral practice of the people of Oceania.

But another reason has been suggested to explain the hammerhead shark's popularity as a tattoo design: It could simply be because it is beautiful!

Coral

Sometimes huge, some coral colonies are several hundred or even several thousand years old.

Coral is an animal. More specifically, it is a colony of small organisms called "polyps," which build their skeletons over time. Polyps are like very small anemones that eat plankton. Most of them have established a complex and vital collaboration with microscopic algae that allows them to eat and grow. Their strength is clearly in unity—some colonies are 5,000 years old! There are coral of every color and every shape: spheres, columns, anvils, brains, bushes, leaves, and branches. Some can even build themselves into entire reefs, like the Great Barrier Reef in Australia.

On some nights, a few days after a full moon, a unique phenomenon occurs: The coral release countless eggs into the sea, forming curtains of flakes that rise slowly to the surface. These eggs transform into larvae, traveling in the current with the plankton, then turn into polyps, which will fix on something firm before forming a new colony.

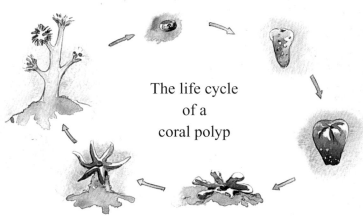

The life cycle of a coral polyp

The eggs and sperm released by coral form larvae, then turn into polyps, which build their skeletons and bud, creating other polyps. Together they form the coral.

It really is an animal!

To reduce pollution (and save coral), limit the amount of time you spend in cars. Walk, ride a bike, or use public transportation instead.

The Great Barrier Reef, one of the biggest coral reefs in the world, is off the coast of Australia.

The situation of coral reefs is cause for major concern. At least half of those still in existence are at risk of disappearing in the coming years. The causes are human activity, pollution, and especially climate change and the resulting increase in water temperatures. Unable to withstand high temperatures, coral expel the microscopic algae they contain and lose their colors. Unable to live without their algae "roommates," they eventually die. The biggest problem is that their disappearance leads to that of countless other organisms, such as the fish, crustaceans, and algae that depend on them to survive.

According to scientists, the only way to save coral is to significantly diminish our greenhouse gas emissions (such as the discharge from car exhausts) and to reduce sea pollution. It has to start at home, because only half of what we throw into our sinks will be purified before reaching watercourses and the sea.

◄ Coral live in symbiosis with algae, which provide them with color, nutrients, and oxygen, thereby allowing a multitude of species to find ideal living conditions.

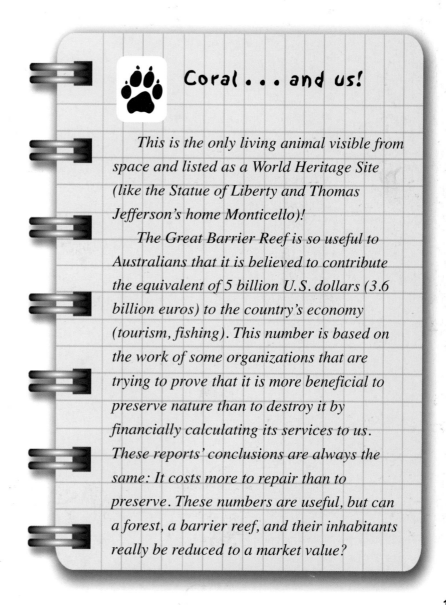

Coral . . . and us!

This is the only living animal visible from space and listed as a World Heritage Site (like the Statue of Liberty and Thomas Jefferson's home Monticello)!

The Great Barrier Reef is so useful to Australians that it is believed to contribute the equivalent of 5 billion U.S. dollars (3.6 billion euros) to the country's economy (tourism, fishing). This number is based on the work of some organizations that are trying to prove that it is more beneficial to preserve nature than to destroy it by financially calculating its services to us. These reports' conclusions are always the same: It costs more to repair than to preserve. These numbers are useful, but can a forest, a barrier reef, and their inhabitants really be reduced to a market value?

The tree kangaroo

The shy tree kangaroo lives in small groups in the humid and mountainous rain forests of Papua New Guinea as well as in Queensland, Australia, and other islands nearby.

Did you know that there are kangaroos that live in trees? This tree kangaroo's hind legs aren't as big as those of its terrestrial kin, but like them, it's a marsupial, which means that mothers carry their young in a ventral pouch throughout their infancy.

To climb trees, tree kangaroos clasp tree trunks with their powerful forepaws and push with their hind legs to propel themselves toward the top, letting their arms slide along the tree trunk. They are real acrobats. Thanks to their large feet and long tails, which they use as balancing poles, they're able to remain perfectly stable when they're perched on a branch, eating delicious pieces of fruit. But they don't spend their entire lives in trees. They often come down to the ground to search for food. And unlike other kangaroos, they're able to walk by alternating the movement of their legs.

Marsupials love to eat leaves and consume copious amounts of them. But they'll also sample grains, insects, eggs, and even some young birds from time to time. They have large stomachs to digest all of that greenery, in a manner similar to cows.

A tree kangaroo in its natural habitat.

An excellent acrobat

Choosing local wood or wood labeled FSC when purchasing an object like a pencil or a table helps preserve forests and their inhabitants.

The tree kangaroo lives in the rain forests of Papua New Guinea at altitudes between 3,200 and 6,500 feet.

This tremendous marsupial is in danger of becoming extinct. While it used to be common throughout Papua New Guinea, it now takes refuge only in mountain forests. The drop in its population is due not only to higher rates of hunting, but especially to deforestation for the exploitation of wood, oil, ore, and the expansion of agriculture. This is not surprising considering that less than half of the original rain forest has survived in this area.

Rain forests are extremely rich in various species. They are home to more than three in four of the species living on dry land. But these sanctuaries are sorely mistreated. If the current rate of deforestation continues, there may no longer be any rain forests in Papua New Guinea in as few as 15 years!

These forests are cleared of trees for wood trade, intensive farming, and palm oil and soya farming. What if we tried to be responsible? For instance, we should make sure the wood we buy was cut in a manner respectful of the forest (certified by the FSC label) and check where the products we consume came from.

◀ The tree kangaroo's long tail serves as a counterweight, which allows it to leap between trees up to 20 feet apart and to let itself drop to the ground from heights of 30 to 65 feet without hurting itself.

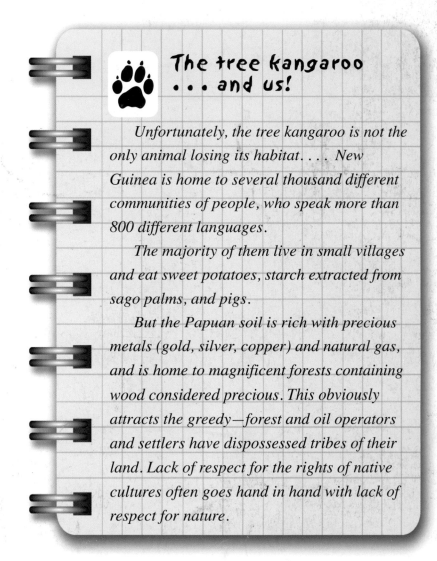

The tree kangaroo . . . and us!

Unfortunately, the tree kangaroo is not the only animal losing its habitat. . . . New Guinea is home to several thousand different communities of people, who speak more than 800 different languages.

The majority of them live in small villages and eat sweet potatoes, starch extracted from sago palms, and pigs.

But the Papuan soil is rich with precious metals (gold, silver, copper) and natural gas, and is home to magnificent forests containing wood considered precious. This obviously attracts the greedy—forest and oil operators and settlers have dispossessed tribes of their land. Lack of respect for the rights of native cultures often goes hand in hand with lack of respect for nature.

The Komodo dragon

The carnivorous Komodo dragon has bones in its skull that are very flexible and that allow its jaws to open incredibly wide to catch its prey. Its sixty curved teeth do the rest of the job.

At 10 feet long, this reptile is the biggest lizard in the world. It's become so enormous because it lives on an island where it is the only predator. Therefore, it has all the food it could wish for, with the needs to match. It's able to eat portions of food equal to 80 percent of its own weight! That's as if a human swallowed 90 pounds of meat in a single sitting! This carnivore, which has no problem feasting on carcasses, goes after prey of all sizes: small invertebrates, birds, and mammals, including deer.

Perched on an overhang of a rocky promontory in the shade of a tree, it spends the hottest hours of the day watching for its prey. Once it has spotted something, it quietly approaches, then leaps onto it and bites. The Komodo dragon doesn't mind if its prey gets away—its bite is lethal. The dragon's mouth contains extremely poisonous bacteria.

Once the prey has been bitten, it will die a few days later from an infection. The dragon just has to wait and use its highly developed sense of smell to find the carcass. It can track it down from up to 6 miles away.

The Komodo dragon is a huge reptile, weighing nearly 220 pounds.

Deadly saliva

We must learn how to consume less and differently. Our consumption is more than what the planet can give us, which doesn't leave much room for other species to live.

The Komodo dragon lives on a handful of small Indonesian islands.

The Komodo dragon has only survived on a handful of small Indonesian islands. Its population has gradually dwindled due to increases in human activities, which have led to the reduction of its habitat and diminished the amount of available prey. Natural disasters such as earthquakes, volcanic activity, and fires have also contributed to the decline of the total population of Komodo dragons in the wild to between 3,000 and 5,000 individuals.

In addition to the Komodo dragon, the most stunning animals live on these islands. Totally isolated from each other, such species, known as "endemic," have evolved separately, each developing their own special characteristics. But since these small pieces of land have a limited surface area, their populations are small and extremely vulnerable. If living conditions become unfavorable, it is impossible for them to escape to find an environment better suited to their needs.

To protect these endemic animal and plant species, we could start by not picking the unknown flowers we encounter and not bringing back "souvenirs" from nature when we go on vacation.

◄ The Komodo dragon primarily uses its long tongue to detect the odor of a rotting carcass. Its tongue even allows it to find its way in the dark. Its sense of taste, however, is very limited.

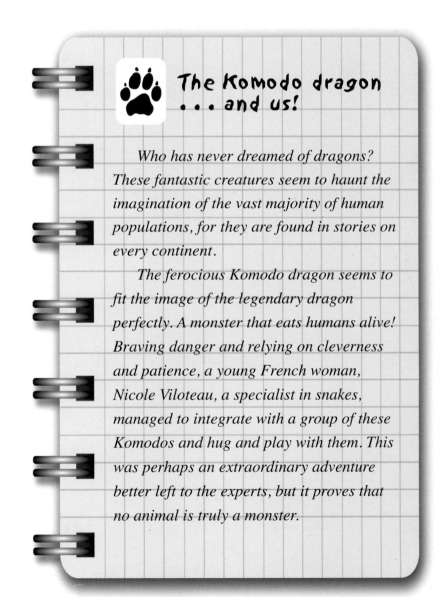

The Komodo dragon ... and us!

Who has never dreamed of dragons? These fantastic creatures seem to haunt the imagination of the vast majority of human populations, for they are found in stories on every continent.

The ferocious Komodo dragon seems to fit the image of the legendary dragon perfectly. A monster that eats humans alive! Braving danger and relying on cleverness and patience, a young French woman, Nicole Viloteau, a specialist in snakes, managed to integrate with a group of these Komodos and hug and play with them. This was perhaps an extraordinary adventure better left to the experts, but it proves that no animal is truly a monster.

147

The New Caledonia flying fox

Though it is still possible to witness large groups of New Caledonia flying foxes, the species is truly endangered. Meanwhile, within a colony it is sometimes difficult for flying foxes to find a spot to sleep, which leads to hours of squabbling!

Bats are the only flying mammals. There are two types of bats: small bats, which have a famous sonar (a highly developed sensory system that allows them to find their way in the dark by emitting sounds and listening to their echo), and flying foxes, which are big and can easily find their way with their large eyes, which provide better vision. With a far more appealing profile than their smaller fellow bats, flying foxes' heads are reminiscent of a fox's, which is where they get their name.

About the size of a seagull, flying foxes are imposing bats that live in New Caledonia. During the day, they sleep in groups in tall trees in remote areas with males and females in separate camps.

At dusk, the flying foxes soar off in large groups in search of their favorite food: fruits and flowers.

The flying fox's wings consist of a membrane extending between its hind paws and its forepaws, which have unusually large phalanges.

A flying fox with big eyes

The flying fox is a central animal in Kanak culture. This is why traditional hunters must also learn not to endanger the species.

The tall trees of New Caledonia are home to the New Caledonia flying fox.

This flying fox has long been hunted for its meat, which is savored by the people of New Caledonia. In order to limit the damage from overhunting, selling flying fox meat has been banned. Though some hunting is still authorized, it is regulated. It can take place only during certain times of year and according to a specific schedule. Additionally, each hunter is allowed to catch only a few flying foxes per day and can hunt them only outside of the areas where they sleep. Still, despite these measures, the number of flying foxes continues to drop.

The case of the flying fox is emblematic of the problems raised by hunting. So long as humans killed only what they needed to eat, species did not suffer. But firearms were developed and, with them, a type of hunting that kills far more animals, sometimes indiscriminately. There are laws to prevent hunters from killing more animals than a species can tolerate. Hunters must therefore learn to recognize these species. But there are many, many more reasons for knowing animals than just that.

◀ The New Caledonia blossom bat has a similar appearance to its cousin, the flying fox. They also share certain traits, such as being born blind, hairless, and toothless, but with the knowledge of how to grip onto their mothers' hairs during nocturnal flights.

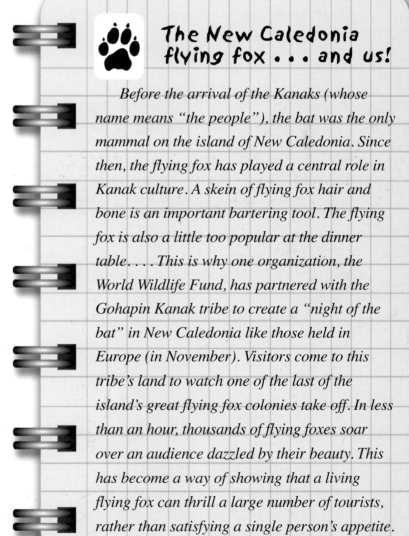

The New Caledonia flying fox . . . and us!

Before the arrival of the Kanaks (whose name means "the people"), the bat was the only mammal on the island of New Caledonia. Since then, the flying fox has played a central role in Kanak culture. A skein of flying fox hair and bone is an important bartering tool. The flying fox is also a little too popular at the dinner table. . . . This is why one organization, the World Wildlife Fund, has partnered with the Gohapin Kanak tribe to create a "night of the bat" in New Caledonia like those held in Europe (in November). Visitors come to this tribe's land to watch one of the last of the island's great flying fox colonies take off. In less than an hour, thousands of flying foxes soar over an audience dazzled by their beauty. This has become a way of showing that a living flying fox can thrill a large number of tourists, rather than satisfying a single person's appetite.

Glossary

Below is a list of terms and their definitions to help you better understand animals and their environment.

Adaptation: *the result of a species' evolution to better conform to its surroundings in order to survive.*

Biodiversity: *the range of living beings.*

Carnivore: *an animal that eats meat.*

Climate change: *alterations in weather patterns and average temperatures, many of which are due to human activity.*

Diet: *the food that an animal eats.*

Domestication: *the result of a wild species being taught by humans to function within human constraints, whether as a pet or a working animal.*

Ecosystem: *a community of living beings and the environment in which they live.*

Ecotourism: *a type of recreational travel based on the observation and respect of nature.*

Endemic: *native to or existing only in a highly localized area.*

Environment: *the overall structure of natural elements that constitute a habitat.*

Food chain: *the sequence of living beings relying on each other for food.*

Gene: *the part of a DNA strand that carries a specific characteristic through heredity.*

Habitat: *the place in which a species lives.*

Herbivore: *an animal that eats plants.*

Mammal: *the category of warm-blooded, vertebrate animals are covered in fur and whose young are nourished with their mothers' milk.*

Microloan: *a small amount of money loaned to impoverished individuals in order to allow them to develop things like wells and grain mills.*

Omnivore: *a living being—like a human—that eats many kinds of food, including both animals and plants.*

Poaching: *illegal hunting.*

Predator: *an animal that hunts other animals for food.*

Reintroduction: *placing a species back into an environment from which it had originally disappeared.*

Species: *a category of living beings that can interbreed.*

Tropical rain forest: *a forest growing near the equator, where it is hot and humid all year long.*

Index

How you can help endangered animals

It is urgent that we protect and care for nature, animals, and plants all around the world. There are many ways you can help, from the comfort of your own home to getting involved with your community. Here are a few suggestions on how to get started:

Sponsor an endangered animal

Create a habitat for animals

Recycle, reduce, and reuse

Let your voice be heard

Get creative!

Sponsor an endangered animal

There are many organizations (for example, the World Wildlife Fund) that will allow you to adopt an endangered animal, like a tiger or a panda. There may even be organizations set up in your own town. When you donate, your support helps raise funds for conservation efforts. If you adopt an animal, you can choose which one you'd like to help and at which cost. In many cases, you'll get an adoption certificate and a photograph of the animal you've helped sponsor as a token of appreciation.

Create a habitat for animals

You can help animals by creating a natural habitat in your very own backyard! Ask your parents to help you make a garden. Plant flowers and shrubs that are native to your geographic area so that they will attract native birds, insects, and other species. Hang a bird feeder and set up a birdbath as well, and watch nature flourish from your own windows.

Recycle, reduce, and reuse

Rather than throwing away everything you consume, start recycling at home. Plastic bottles, glass containers, and paper can all be recycled, which allows us to reuse discarded materials. Recycling not only cuts down on pollution, but it also benefits wildlife by preserving natural habitats. Recycling is an easy and efficient way to help the environment without having to leave your home. Save energy by turning off lights and the television when you're not using them. Don't leave the water running while you brush your teeth. Ride your bike or take the bus to school. Donate old clothes and toys to organizations. The possibilities are endless!

Let your voice be heard

Find out who your state senators and representatives are (ask your parents or your teachers for help with getting this information), and then write to them about your concerns, whether it's animals or the environment. Create a petition that specifically voices your concerns and then share it with your neighbors to sign before you send it to your state senators. Write a letter to your local newspaper. No matter how you ultimately voice your opinion, you can raise awareness on these very important issues.

Get creative!

Saving endangered animals and the environment is a serious and important concern, but that doesn't mean you can't have some fun, too, to raise awareness. Choose your favorite endangered animals and draw pictures, create masks to wear, make puppets, write a story or a play to perform, and read more books about endangered animals. What is most important is that you share your knowledge and information with everyone around you. Encourage others to research endangered animals, so that we can all be aware of the risks they face and how we can help protect them.